HEALING TEAS
from
AROUND *the* WORLD

HEALING TEAS
from
AROUND *the* WORLD

By Sylvia Schneider

With a Foreword by Terry Willard CI.H, Ph.D

SARASOTA PRESS

National Library of Canada Cataloguing in Publication Data
Schneider, Sylvia
   Healing teas from around the world

Translation of: Tees aus aller Welt.
ISBN 1-55356-009-4

   1. Herbal teas–Therapeutic use. I. Title.

RM666.H33S35 2001   615'.321
C2001-901104-0

Published in the United States in 2001 by
Sarasota Press
an imprint of Key Porter Books Limited
4808 South Tamiami Trail
PMB #205
Sarasota, Florida
34231-4352

Published in Canada in 2001 by
Key Porter Books Limited
70 The Esplanade
Toronto, Ontario
Canada M5E 1R4

Originally published in German in 1998 by Mosaik Verlag, GmgH, Munich

www.keyporter.com

Photography: Wolf-Dieter Böttcher
Food Styling: Helge Stüssel-Harzer
Electronic formatting: Jean Peters

Publisher's Note: The contents of this book are not intended to be used as a substitution for consultation with your physician. All matters pertaining to your health should be directed to a health care professional.

Printed and bound in Spain

01 02 03 04 05 6 5 4 3 2 1

CONTENTS

FOREWORD

Herbs are the primary form of medicine for over 80% of the world's population, according to the United Nation's World Health Organization. Here in North America we are enjoying a resurgence and renewed interest in botanical medicines. In this beautiful book, translated from German, Sylvia Schneider takes us on a wonderful journey around the world, peering over the shoulders of traditional healers to look at some of their most famous formulas. Teas have been enjoyed by people from the beginning of human civilization and are still the most common way to administer botanical remedies today.

Schneider's journey begins with an Asian experience; looking at the teas of China, Japan, India and Tibet. We learn how these formulas have been prepared, so we can appreciate their influences, while bringing their exotic smells and flavors right in our own home. From here we journey to the Middle East, Latin America and Europe to gain a deeper flavor of the medicinal teas of those regions.

From teas that will calm, to teas that will strengthen, you, your friends and family will surely find this book an enjoyable and informative guide. Browsing through these pages you will find formulas from the famous saint Hildegard von Bingen to the Tibetan masters. As a practising Clinical Herbalist since 1975, I have traveled the world extensively searching for information and sources of herbal remedies. In this volume, I find a wealth of information covering traditions as diverse as Ayurvedic medicines from India, Shamanistic preparations from the Amazon and modern European manufacturing techniques. In this elegant compilation of tea knowledge from around the world, you are sure to find material that will interest you.

Many explorers and trade delegations throughout history went out to search the world for rare herbs and spices to heal their nation's people. This book makes your ventures much easier and convenient. So, brew a cup of your favorite herbal tea, curl up with this beautifully photographed book, and start on a new adventure of tastes, smells and temptations.

Terry Willard Cl.H, Ph.D.
May 2001, Calgary, Alberta

INTRODUCTION
Dew from Heaven: Appreciating a Cup of Tea

"This draft is dew that falls from Heaven, light and mild. You call it Tea!"

from the annals of the Sung dynasty

Tea has magical powers. Tea consoles the lonely and unites the sociable. Tea stimulates in hot countries and heats the body where it is cold. Tea can alleviate or heal ailments of the body and the soul. Tea drinking is a many-faceted pleasure: it can cause us to dream, sharpen our minds, relax us, let us forget time and place, and heal our body, mind and soul. The ceremony of tea drinking is associated with warmth, pleasant fragrances and comfort. Tea seduces the senses. In these days of stress and hurry, more and more of us seek peace and contemplation in a cup of tea. The number of tea drinkers is growing.

Preparing tea from an amazing variety of plants has a long, long history, as does the tradition of using tea for meditative and spiritual purposes. The use of tea in the contemplative life was known to the sages of the Far East, the physicians of Arabia, the priests of ancient Egypt, the shamans of the North American Indians and of the rain forests, and the wise women of Europe. From the beginning, tea has served not just as a beverage but also as medicine. And tea carries with it the philosophy of all those who have brewed it and prescribed it. For these reasons, teas made of magic herbs offer a very special form of pleasure. They are messengers from the place of their origin and they tell us about history, lost civilizations, unknown cultures, forgotten customs, women's lore, erotica and exotica.

"It will never be discovered how human beings happened upon the pleasure of hot

infusions, made of the leaves of a certain shrub or of the roasted and boiled seeds of another. Yet there must be an explanation for how these infusions became a vital necessity in the lives of entire nations. Even more amazing is the fact—which the wildest imagination could never have thought of—that we must ascribe their beneficial effect upon the human body to the exact same chemical component in both plants. Yet they happen to belong to entirely different botanical families and stem from two different continents." Thus wrote Justus Liebig about tea and coffee in 1842, in his groundbreaking work on organic chemistry, physiology and pathology.

What are the healing powers of the myriad herbs and spices that have been used in all parts of the world to prepare teas, some fragrant and enchanting, others bitter? Recently, scientific research has begun to document the beneficial qualities of many herbs. Their virtues were known long ago, however, and many herbs had spread far and wide even in ancient times, so that today the same or similar plants can be found on most continents. This attests to the significance herbs have had for people everywhere. Herbs know no borders; their universality is their essence.

In this book you will find remedies, herbs and spices that come from East and West, from both the New World and the Old. Everywhere, even in the remotest corners of the globe, herbs have always existed, unfolding their magic aura and drawing men and women under their spell. We carefully followed the trails of ancient magical herbs and recipes to spiritual healers, physicians and shamans of various cultures, whose families have employed them for generations. The recipes were then submitted to various critical tests and, where necessary, adapted to the

needs of our modern urban lifestyle. We focused on those teas that can be either obtained in prepared form or prepared with ingredients that are easy to procure. In this process we were able to take into account all the latest scientific research on herbs and their effects, giving you concrete information about both the relationship of herbs to illnesses and everyday complaints and the influence of healing herbs on beauty and well-being.

In addition to the many recipes, this beautifully designed book will give you countless hours of interesting reading about the history, customs and ideas of the different cultures that were originally responsible for making the teas in this book. We hope that this will induce you to try the magic powers of tea for yourself, and to experience the world in a cup of dew from heaven.

Sylvia Schneider
January 1998

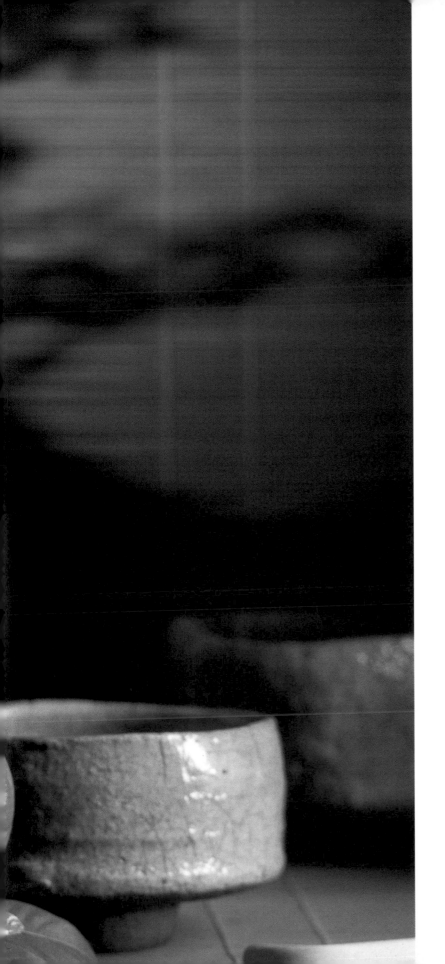

ASIA

STORIES FROM THE FAR EAST
How the Wisdom of Asia Reached Europe

What is it about Asia that so enchants us? It has been a good twenty years since the latest Far Eastern cultural wave hit our shores and carried us away, and there is no end in sight. On the contrary: after a short ebb, it seems to overwhelm us again, like a spring tide. Decades ago Asia stopped being the reserve of globetrotters and spiritual seekers. Asia is now mainstream. Asia is everywhere. Asia is in the chic sushi bar, in fashionable slicked-down hair, white makeup and cherry red mouth, in sake baths and algae-based cosmetics. Asia is in our apartments designed using feng shui, and in the ubiquitous futon. Asia is in our heads. And that is probably a good thing.

Since the West has been sinking into a stressful morass, we have been looking to the East for solutions. And there we find things that fascinate us. We find an attitude that emphasizes mindfulness and humility. We find a spirituality that teaches awe and meditation, emptiness instead of glut, discipline instead of excess, gratitude instead of arrogance, modesty instead of greed. In a word, detachment.

Deep within our being, we esteem the East. "You are what you eat," says the Asian. We have heard this cliché so often that we forget that it originated in Asia, where for thousands of years food has been used as medicine.

Far Eastern medicine appeals to us. Fascinated by the Ayurvedic tradition of ancient India, we submit to complete cleansing programs, which free the body of poisons and waste products, and offer meditation and contemplation into the bargain. China too has arrived. Tai Chi and Qi Gong, the great traditions of meditative movement from the Middle Kingdom, are taught in our community centers.

More and more doctors and health practitioners include Chinese methods in their repertoire. Asian herbs are the fastest sellers in herbal and Oriental supply houses. Museums present Japanese tea rituals. Japanese medicine is by now so common that we take it for granted. Acupressure, the healing pressure-massage of the meridian points, was developed by Japanese doctors. In the better spas, acupressure is a routine part of beauty treatments. Shiatsu may well be the most relaxing form of physical therapy; every last bit of stress is worked out of muscles, tendons and the very whorls of the brain by the pushing, stretching and stroking hands of the practitioner. And remember, shiatsu is a part of Japanese medicine.

At the moment, we are particularly taken by Tibetan healing methods. Recent movies have opened up to us the history of the Tibetan people, and we are receiving teachings from this distant country, where Buddhism is aligned with healing as in no other place on earth. Buddhism itself has become a revelation for many Westerners. It offers us a new combination: good cheer and detachment. Who knows, we may be turning towards Asia just to catch a glimpse of the Buddha's smile!

Chinese medicine classifies fruits and vegetables according to the five elements: kiwi fruit stands for wood, the pomegranate represents fire, the pear symbolizes earth, apple metal, and the edible chestnut, water.

CHINA
HEALING LORE FROM THE MIDDLE KINGDOM

Traditional Chinese Medicine (TCM) is probably the oldest medical system in use today. It originated more than six thousand years ago. About 200 BC, its principles were recorded in the *Principles of Internal medicine* of the Yellow Emperor.

Chinese healers regard the human being as part of a cosmic system. By its very nature, this regulatory system is constantly maintaining a stable equilibrium, or homeostasis. Disturbance in one's relation to the environment, as well as illness, is seen as energy that has moved out of equilibrium. Healing involves getting the energy once more into alignment with the harmonious whole.

The Five Elements

From time immemorial the Chinese have classified the phenomena of this world into five metaphysical elements: Wood, Fire, Earth, Metal and Water. All natural processes are determined by the interplay of these basic forces. Each of the elements also exerts a stimulating or suppressive force on one of the other elements and is in turn aided or hindered by another one. This interaction of elements can be seen as follows: in Stimulation there is a sequential production, in that Wood can burn and produce Fire, which produces ash, which in turn becomes Earth. Earth can be transformed into Metal, which is taken from it. Metal can melt and flow like Water. Water causes plants to grow, thus producing Wood. The Inhibition cycle of interaction produces sequential checks: Wood can suppress Earth in that plants can invade and deplete the earth's nutrients. Earth in turn can suppress Water by absorbing it. Water can suppress or impede Fire by putting it out. Fire can suppress

Metal by melting it, and Metal can cut Wood.

The five elements and their positive and negative interactions apply to all of nature and also within individual men and women; they apply to the human body, emotions, actions and sounds. All the organs and functions of the body are seen as expressions of this interacting set of five elements.

Although at first this approach to healing may seem strange, its results are often supported by Western medicine. Thus traditional Chinese medicine regards the liver as expressing Wood, and associates muscles, eyes and nails with the liver. Western doctors also know of these connections. TCM further states that the emotions of anger and depression are associated with the liver, and Western doctors are aware that patients with liver disease or weakness are subject to violent fits of rage that alternate with periods of depression. However, because they focus on the interaction of the elements with the organs, Chinese doctors are far better when it comes to recognizing and treating the physical basis of psychological syndromes. To use the example cited above, TCM can frequently cure depression because it addresses the liver, not the symptomatic depression.

Yin and Yang

Another basic tenet of TCM is the complementary polarity of Yin and Yang. Balance is the aim of therapy with respect to Yin and Yang as well. Yin is quiescent while Yang is active. The entire universe is seen as a constantly changing equilibrium between these two qualities.

The Meridians

The meridians are energy paths that course throughout the body. Qi, the life force, flows through the meridians to the major organs that lie along their paths. When the qi is free to move, it promotes the harmonious functioning of the whole system. The most important meridians are associated with the heart, kidneys and lungs. According to Asian medicine, external forces can reach and flow along the meridians, but dysfunction too can spread along the meridian from a diseased organ. This is why so-called "Stomach Fire" can cause gum disease, and "Gallbladder Fire" can lead to problems with the ears.

The Pillars of Chinese Medicine

Traditional Chinese Medicine rests on five pillars:

- acupuncture and Moxa therapies
- *tuina* massage and chiropractic
- movement and breath therapy, such as Tai Chi and Qi Gong
- nutrition
- healing herbal therapy, which includes minerals and some animal products

Practicing Chinese herbal therapy in the West is still relatively difficult. Although Chinese herbalists use some plants available here, such as blackberry, catnip, garlic and plantain, different plant parts are usually used, and often different varieties as well. Many plants that grow only in China are still difficult to obtain, especially for non-professionals. A major reason is that healing herbs are subject to the very strict laws that govern all medical substances, their use and import.

Chinese importers have begun to declare Chinese herbs as foods rather than drugs. This practice—in addition to simplifying the process of clearing these plants through customs—is in harmony with the view that "food is medicine, medicine is food." In fact, a decoction—a plant essence obtained by boiling—is called *tang*, and that word also means soup. Chinese decoctions, or herbal soups, are produced by reducing the water in which the ingredients are simmered to one-quarter of the original volume. Rice may be added to the *tang* to produce a mushy, healing meal. Thus, the Chinese use their herbal remedies simultaneously for healing, enjoyment and nourishment.

Chinese cooking always strives to offer each person what his constitution and current state of health requires. This usually happens in the home. In Chengdu, however, there is a special restaurant situated beside the premises of a herbal doctor. A customer visits the health practitioner, obtains a recipe, and then hands it to the head waiter when she arrives at the restaurant. The chef then prepares a meal according to the principles of TCM, in which he is formally trained.

THE ESSENTIAL HERBS OF CHINESE MEDICINE

Through the knowledge of healers accumulated over the millennia, Chinese herbal medicine has become a very complex subject. The medical application of plants is first of all governed by their relationship to the five elements. Then the herbalist bases his particular choice of plant on its taste, smell, form and color, the configuration of its fruit, and even its habitat. A Chinese doctor has a repertoire of over a thousand plants to choose from. What follows is a small selection.

Astragalus Root

Astragalus membranaceus Chinese astragalus is a relative of the milk vetch, a group of plants known as *huang qi*. The plant grows mostly in northern China, Mongolia and Manchuria. Astragalus root is classified as sweet and slightly warm by Chinese medicine, is a significant energy tonic, and is used primarily to strengthen the immune system. Its effects are diuretic: it increases the elimination of urine, although it reduces sweating. Decoctions of astragalus root have a wide range of applications. Chinese doctors use the plant in cases of low energy, fatigue, excessive perspiration due to certain deficiencies, facial edemas, abscesses, and even diabetes and uterine prolapse.

Chinese Wolfberry

Lycium chinense The Chinese wolfberry, a nightshade widespread in China and Japan, is known as *digupi* in Chinese. *Digupi* refers to the skin of the root, which is classified as sweet and cold and is used in treating the lungs, liver and kidneys. In cases of "excessive heat in the lungs," such as asthma, coughing and spitting blood, *digupi* is particularly effective.

The ripe fruit of the Chinese wolfberry, which is also used, is called *goukizi. Goukizi*, sweet and neither warm nor cold, is a tonic for the liver and kidneys. It is prescribed against yin-deficiencies. A liver yin-deficiency will cause blurred vision, vertigo and headaches, and in the kidneys yin-deficiency can lead to spermatorrhea, the loss of sperm without sexual stimulation.

Chinese Angelica

Angelica Sinensis *Dong quai* or *danggui* is a lovely, umbel-bearing herb that grows wild all over central Asia. Related to the Western angelica, the plant is probably the most important remedy used by women in Chinese medicine, although men take it as well. What is used is the root, which is regarded as sweet and acrid, and warm. It especially affects the heart, liver and spleen. *Danggui* balances the hormones that regulate the monthly cycle, calms the organs of reproduction and can improve their functioning. Chinese physicians prescribe raw *danggui* to relax the womb and to lessen menstrual pain. Mixed with water, the *danggui* root stimulates uterine contractions and increases blood flow. This effect is employed to restore menstruation in young women when it has stopped or become irregular. After giving birth, Chinese women are aided in their recovery by *danggui*. The effects of this root on blood circulation is stimulating and toning. Overall, it acts as an analgesic, sedative and laxative.

Chrysanthemum

Chrysanthemum morifolium The Chinese healing chrysanthemum is related to the decorative plant we value for its large flowers, but it is not the same. *Juhau* is the Chinese name of the plant, of which only the flower is used. Its qualities are bitter and acrid as well as cool. It has an affinity for the lungs and liver. Chrysanthemum helps in cooling fevers, improving vision, eliminating poisons, lowering blood pressure and generally in calming and cooling. It is employed against headaches, the so-called "Wind and Heat" diseases, swellings and eye strain. A compress of chrysanthemum tea will soothe the eyes of a person suffering from conjunctivitis.

Ginseng

Panax Ginseng, the root shaped like a man, is one of the oldest tonics in the world. For over five thousand years the Chinese have relied on the power of this "royal" root as the supreme healing plant. Ever since Louis XIV's time Westerners too have used the root to treat exhaustion and weakness and to prolong life.

There are several varieties of ginseng, among them the variety cultivated in the United States, *Panax quinquefolius*, and the Chinese *Panax notoginseng*. The most expensive, valuable and effective, however, is *Panax ginseng*, known as Korean or Chinese ginseng. It is cultivated in northeastern China (Manchuria) and in Korea. Scientific research done in the West has proven that ginseng strengthens the immune system. Science has also shown that *Panax ginseng* contains steroid-like components that resemble human sexual hormones.

The cultivation of ginseng requires long, labor-intensive care. Only after six years of growth is the root ready to be harvested. In Asia ginseng is not only the most frequently used medicine, but it is enjoyed in other ways too. It is used as a spice and consumed as tea. Pieces of ginseng root can be chewed for

hours, like chewing gum. In the West ginseng is usually available as a powder, in capsules or as a liquid tonic.

All these forms of the plant serve the same purpose: to strengthen sexual potency and vitality, to counteract arteriosclerosis and to lessen the symptoms of aging in general. In terms of efficacy, extracts, both liquid and powdered, carry the most concentrated power and impact. Pure ginseng extract is a thick syrup that can be taken straight or diluted with hot water, as a tea. Powdered and granulated ginseng extracts seem to have an especially intensive aroma. They are best enjoyed as a tea, possibly sweetened with honey.

Warning: Pregnant women and anyone suffering from high blood pressure should avoid high dosages of ginseng as well as ingestion of the root over prolonged periods of time. In general, during ginseng therapy, other stimulants, such as coffee, tea or cola beverages, should be avoided.

Senna, or Cassia Tree

Cassia tora This plant is called *juemingzi* in China. It grows in the south of that country and in Indochina, India and Southeast Asia. Chinese medicine uses the seeds, which are sweet, bitter and salty, and cool, and associates cassia with the liver and the gallbladder. The uses of the plant are therefore directed at complaints that directly or indirectly arise from disturbances of these two organs. Swollen and inflamed eyes, a result of overheated liver, and excessive sensitivity to light are prime examples. Contemporary physicians also employ cassia against high blood pressure and high blood cholesterol levels. Cassia is best known, how-

ever, as a laxative, mostly used in cases of chronic constipation. The leaves and seeds of the tree affect the intestines and yield the active ingredient senna, which lends its name to the tree itself. These parts of the plants are also used in some Chinese weight-loss teas because they stimulate the digestion and the intestinal tract. (See Ning-Hong Slimming Tea on page 18.)

Peony

Paeonia Reduced to the function of an ornamental perennial in the West, the peony plays a very important role in China: it is regarded as the symbol of Chinese medicine. Two major varieties are used: *Paeonia lactiflora*, which blooms red and white and bears the name Chinese peony, and the tree peony, *Paeonia suffruticosa*. Only the roots or the skin of the roots are used.

The root of the red-blooming *Paeonia lactiflora*, *chishaoyao*, cools the blood, moves stagnant blood to reduce swelling, and alleviates pain. It is said that this plant lowers blood pressure, reduces inflammation and loosens cramps, as well as being an antibacterial agent. In conjunction with other herbs, this variety of peony is very successful in curing eczema in children. The white-blooming variety of *Paeonia lactiflora*, known as *baishaoyao*, is used in connection with malfunctions of the liver and as a tonic for menstrual difficulties. A decoction of *baishaoyao* with licorice improves the complexion: simmer 0.7 oz. (20 g) *baishaoyao* with 0.2 oz. (5 g) licorice in 2 cups (500 ml) water for 15 minutes over low heat, and drink 2 cups a day.

Only the skin on the root of the tree peony, *mudanpi*, is used in Chinese medicine. This antibacterial and anti-inflammatory agent also lowers blood pressure and stimulates the circulation. This peony variety serves through its blood-cooling abilities to reduce fevers and through its antibacterial qualities to clear up purulent dermatitis.

Schisandra

Schisandra chinensis The schisandra tree grows in Japan and China. Its dried fruit (*wuweizi*) has a regulatory effect on the metabolism and on blood pressure. Coughing and chronic asthma may also be treated with a decoction of schisandra fruit. The regulatory virtue of this plant is so generally effective that it acts as a diuretic in cases where too much fluid is retained in the system and retains water when organs and mucus tissues are too dry.

THE BEST CHINESE TEA RECIPES FOR BEAUTY, HEALTH AND WELL-BEING

The Ning Hong Healing teas, which have recently become available in North American health food stores, are famous in China for their general efficacy. There are two versions, and both consist of 50 percent Ning Hong tea, considered by Chinese tea specialists to be the best black tea grown in China. (See back of book for list of suppliers.)

Ning Hong Tea for Men

Though called a tea for men, this highly valued tonic is equally effective for women. In truth, it serves as a source of energy for anyone who takes it. It delivers a genuine energy boost, while its toxicity has been proved to be less than that of commercial black tea. It works by strengthening the kidneys and yang (male) energy. According to Chinese medicine the kidneys are the seat of life energy. In men, strengthening the kidneys can increase sexual potency and fertility. A clinical study done in China showed a 50-percent increase in the sperm count of subjects after only five days of drinking Ning Hong tea for men.

3.5 oz. (100 g) of the tea mixture contains:
1.5 oz. (43 g) Ning Hong Tea
0.8 oz. (22 g) oyster extract
0.5 oz. (15 g) Chinese wolfberry
0.7 oz. (20 g) loquat fruit
(or Japanese medlar)

Preparation and use: Each tea bag yields 3 cups of tea and is steeped 3 times. In the first infusion, 20 percent of the ingredients are dissolved, in the second, 60 percent and in the third, 20 percent. To enjoy the tea, place a tea

bag into a cup and pour hot water over it. Let it steep for 5 minutes and drink the tea. Replace the tea bag in the cup, pour water over it, let steep 5 minutes and drink the tea again, right away. Repeat this procedure once more. Drink 3 cups of the tea 3 times each day, before meals. That makes 9 cups altogether per day.

Ning Hong Slimming Tea

Glowing reports reach us concerning this diet tea from China. About one thousand obese patients from three different hospitals drank the tea over a long period, three times a day. Their diet was low on sugar and meat, but otherwise normal. Ninety-five percent of subjects lost significant amounts of weight. Detailed studies show that regular use of the Ning Hong slimming tea stimulates digestion and cures heartburn and bad breath. It is also prescribed for patients with high blood pressure, high cholesterol, diabetes and cardiovascular diseases. These complaints are often associated with obesity. The tea can be taken as part of a weight-loss diet or enjoyed in its own right.

3.5 oz. (100 g) of the tea mixture contains:
2 oz. (56 g) Ning Hong tea
0.6 oz. (18 g) cassia
0.4 oz. (12 g) camomile
0.3 oz. (9 g) azarole (or Neapolitan medlar)
0.1 oz. (3 g) lujiaojiao (a gelatin extracted from deer antlers)
0.1 oz. (2 g) licorice

Preparation and use: Exactly as with the tea for men, each tea bag is steeped 3 times. The 3

The energy root, ginseng, is the life elixir of the Asians.

cups of tea are drunk before meals, one after the other. Total tea consumption is 9 cups per day. ***Note to this recipe:*** Ning Hong slimming tea has been awarded several international prizes as a first-class diet product.

Green Healing Teas

The following three recipes have effects similar to the Ning Hong teas, but they are based on green rather than black tea.

Lady Beauty Tea

Chinese ladies swear by this ancient and classic beauty aid for women. This beauty tea is supposed to work by increasing the circulation in the facial capillaries, thus making the skin appear younger, fresher and rosier. Kidney function is also increased by it. Menopausal women will benefit from the hormone-like components of Lady Beauty tea because they stimulate the female libido.

3.5 oz. (100 g) of the tea mixture contains:
1.4 oz. (39.9 g) Longjing green tea
0.4 oz. (10 g) Chinese wolfberry
1.8 oz. (50.1 g) ground lotus seeds

Preparation and use: Unlike the Ning Hong teas, this green tea is steeped only once. Using 1 tea bag, fill the cup with hot water, let it steep for about 5 minutes, and enjoy. To produce visible results, it is best to drink the tea daily for long periods. Chinese women drink the tea early in the morning, after rising, and after each meal. Drinking 3 to 6 cups a day is recommended.

Note to this recipe: The name Longjing refers to the area where this green tea is cultivated, namely the province of Zhejiang. Its capital is the city of Hangzhou.

Black Dragon Tea for Men

This men's tea is a revitalizer for both men and women. It is a gentle alternative for those who cannot tolerate black tea.

3.5 oz. (100 g) of tea mixture contains:
1.6 oz. (46.5 g) Black Dragon tea
0.5 oz. (13.3 g) camomile
1.4 oz. (40.2 g) green beans

Preparation and use: This green tea for men is steeped only once. Pour a cup of hot water over the tea bag and allow to steep for 5 minutes. Drink 3 or 4 cups per day to benefit from this energy source, after meals and perhaps before retiring.

Green Diet Tea

This weight-loss tea can be used as the sole means of regulating one's weight or it can be combined with a diet. Cassia, known also as senna, is a Chinese healing herb. Its seeds deliver most of the punch of this tea. Cassia seeds strongly stimulate the intestines. In other words, this tea speeds up the digestion and processing of food. People who have used this tea report eating normally but losing weight anyway, gradually and steadily. The jasmine tea listed among the ingredients is a green tea enhanced with jasmine.

For 3.5 oz. (100 g) of tea mixture:
1.7 oz. (49.6 g) jasmine tea

0.6 oz. (16.6 g) cassia
1.2 oz. (33.8 g) ground green beans

Preparation and use: A tea bag is infused with boiling water and is allowed to steep for five minutes. Drink 1 or 2 cups before each meal, that is, 3 to 6 cups per day.

Tea Made of Ginseng Extract

One of the greatest gifts of Chinese medicine is this tea made of the "root of energy," ginseng, which strengthens the immune system. Along with valuable vitamins, minerals and fatty acids, we imbibe the treasured ginsenosides, which have a very special quality: they locate and start healing—all by themselves—whatever weak points our body happens to have. Since the efficacy of these ginsensides varies directly with their concentration, it pays to purchase the highly concentrated and expensive extracts.

3 g granulated extract or 1 g syrup extract
1 cup (¼ l) hot water

Preparation and use: Put the granules or syrup into a cup and fill with hot water. To maintain and strengthen the immune system in general, 1 cup a day is sufficient. Take it before a meal. In situations of stress, the dose can be doubled for short periods. If the intense taste of ginseng is too much for you, feel free to sweeten the tea.

Note to this recipe: There is a big difference between ginseng extract and ginseng tea, which is often sold as an instant tea powder or as tea granules. These instant teas are much cheaper than the ginseng extract, but that is because many of these teas contain little ginseng, being

stretched with grape sugar or lactose. The impact of the prepared teas is quite mild, though they can be enjoyed as such, if one relies on another form of ginseng for effect, i.e., capsules or a tonic.

Fertility Tea for Women

Many women with an irregular cycle have problems conceiving. This tea is for them. It will regulate the monthly cycle, strengthen and harmonize the sexual organs, and give a lift to the general energy level of anyone who takes it regularly.

Lady's mantle (Alchemilla vulgaris*)*
False unicorn (Chamaelirium luteum*)*
Chinese angelica (Angelica sinensis*)*
Ginger
Wild yam root
Raspberry leaves
Dried root of licorice

Preparation and use: First you make a mixture: combine the first six herbs in equal quantities by weight. This constitutes one half; the other half is made up of licorice root. Combine the whole mixture very well. Now use only 1 teaspoon per cup. Infuse with 4 oz. (100 ml) water. This is the daily dose, which you can spread over the whole day, sipping small amounts. Do this over several months, till your cycle is normal.

Note to this recipe: Some of the herbs used in this recipe contain phytoestrogens, used for centuries to support the organs of reproduction. Till twenty years ago the wild yam was still used in the production of the birth control pill. Traditionally, the root is prescribed against

menstrual complaints and problems with the ovaries and the uterus. The false unicorn has similar applications, especially for the ovaries. It is particularly helpful in cases of infertility that are the result of faulty follicle production in the ovaries.

The Recipes of the Chinese Professor

The following recipes were created especially for this book by the president of the Academy of Natural Chinese Medicine, Professor Dietmar Kummer. He has served since 1990 as

professor of Chinese medicine at the University of Peking and has been made honorary doctor of the University of Nanking. (The Chinese preparations mentioned in the recipes are available ready-made from a Chinese address listed in the back.)

The Tea of the Hundred-year-old Chinese

In the Barma region of south China there are a large number of centenarians. The rate of cancer is very low there, too. Whatever may be the cause of these statistics, the people of Barma drink Jia-Gu-Lan tea, a variety of green tea, every day.

1 tsp. Jia-Gu-Lan tea per cup of water

Preparation and use: Like any other green tea, this one is brewed with water that has boiled and cooled down to 125–140°F (50° to 60°C). The tea can be sipped over the course of the day. It is said to lower cholesterol levels and prevent the formation of free radicals in the body. The impact of this rejuvenating brew can be intensified by simultaneously taking wuchaseng extract as well.

Jinhua Jasmine Tea

Genuine jasmine teas from China can be amazing; this one happens to bear the name "Lawyers' Tea." It is half-fermented tea, enhanced with some real jasmine blossoms to refine its aroma. It makes an extremely fragrant and tasty beverage for daily enjoyment. In China it is considered a tonic for overall health. The delicate leaves of green tea are the active ingredient.

2 tsp. Jinhua jasmine tea
A pot of hot water
Optional: *a little ginseng extract*

Preparation and use: Place 2 teaspoons of Jinhua jasmine tea into a teapot and add water that has boiled and cooled down a bit. Let it steep for 20 minutes. To add a lift to the spirit, add a few drops of ginseng extract to each cup when you serve it. A cup of this tea morning, noon and night will stimulate memory and vitality.

Power Tea for Men

Chinese medicine identifies many possible causes for male impotence. In cases of kidney-yang weakness this tea is the most helpful.

0.4 oz. (10 g) green grapefruit skin
(Citrus reticulata)
0.1 oz. (3 g) Psoralea corilifolia
0.2 oz. (5 g) Chinese wolfberries
(Lycium chinense)
0.2 oz. (5 g) parsley seeds
1 ¼ cups (300 ml) water

Preparation and use: Bring all ingredients to a slow boil and simmer for 20 minutes, till the liquid is reduced to 3 oz. (100 ml). Strain this medicinal "soup" and sip it through the morning hours. In the afternoon, using the same solid ingredients, add 1 ¼ cups (300 ml) water, repeat the same process of reducing the volume to 3 oz. (100 ml), and drink it very slowly. The same ingredients cannot be kept overnight.

An additional recommendation is to take 2 tablespoons of the Chinese remedy Haima Bu Jiu every morning and before retiring, for 3 months.

The Beauty Tea of the Empresses of China

Legend has it that the empresses of China ate this medicinal soup with red dates to make their skin radiant. The angelica root harmonizes the sexual organs, the dates add glow to the skin, and the Jinhua jasmine tea removes excess water.

0.2 oz. (5 g) Jinhua jasmine tea
0.4 oz. (10 g) Chinese red dates (2 or 3)
0.4 oz. (10 g) Chinese angelica
(Angelica sinensis)
0.2 oz. (5 g) Chinese wolfberries
(Lycium chinense)
1 ¼ cups (300 ml) cold water

Preparation and use: Place all ingredients into the cold water, slowly bring to a boil, and simmer for 20 minutes to reduce the volume to 3 oz. (100 ml). Drink the soup in small sips. In the evening, brew the ingredients again and sip as before.
Warning: The decoction may not be kept overnight; you must make fresh tea every day. Taken daily for 6 weeks, this tea will achieve its full potential. To make it more potent, you can add 1 teaspoon of the female tonic Dang Gui Bei Qi Jiu to each cup.

Tea for Insomnia

One of the basic tenets of Traditional Chinese Medicine is that adequate sleep is needed to balance Yin and Yang. This tea helps with insomnia due to overwork. The Chinese say that this condition will lead to depression, drug and alcohol abuse, and eventually serious illness, characterized by high fevers.

0.4 oz. (12 g) Radix Rehmanniae glutinosae
(root of R. glutinosa)
0.2 oz. (6 g) bunchberry (Cornus officianalis)
0.2 oz. (6 g) Chinese yam (Dioscorea opposita)
0.2 oz. (6 g) Selectorium Poriae cocos
0.2 oz. (6 g) Cortex Moutan radix
0.2 oz. (6 g) Oriental plantain rhyzome
(Alisma orientalis)
1 ¼ cups (300 ml) water

Preparation and use: Bring all ingredients to a short boil and allow to simmer for 20 minutes to reduce liquid to 3 to 4 ½ oz. (100–150 ml). Drink in small sips in the morning and evening. Do not keep the brew overnight.

Men's Tea against Hair Loss

The Chinese know that the tendency to hair loss can be inherited. In any case, it helps to strengthen the scalp. The hair is influenced by the kidneys and the treatment of the blood by the spleen. This recipe can help by nourishing the blood.

0.4 oz. (10 g) knotweed root
0.1 oz. (3 g) stinging nettle seeds
(Urtica) *or dried nettle*
1 tbsp. Taiga ginseng
0.2 oz. (5 g) wolfberries (Lycium chinensis)
0.2 oz. (5 g) ground Eucommia (ulmoides)
1 ¼ cups (300 ml) water

Preparation and use: Prepare a medicinal soup out of these ingredients by simmering them for 20 minutes to reduce the liquid to 3 oz. (100 ml), which you drink. Brew up the same ingredients at night, but do not keep them overnight. It helps to continue taking this tea for

6 weeks. Those who wish to benefit their hair even more can take the Chinese tonic Qi Zi Bu Ji, which contains important nutrients for hair and scalp. For external use, the herbal tincture Hairoka Liniment is recommended. It is most effective against so-called seborrheic baldness, which is most common among men of European origin.

Light Tea for Depression

The Chinese regard depression as resulting from energy blocks (stagnant qi) that affect the spirit. Common causes are anemia due to worry and anxiety, groundless suspicions, sleeplessness and irritability. Against all this, light tea can be effective, if taken along with other therapies.

0.4 oz. (10 g) root of Rehmannia
glutinosa conquita
0.3 oz. (9 g) peony root (Paenia lactiflora)
0.2 oz. (6 g) Chinese angelica root
(Angelica sinensis)
0.2 oz. (6 g) root of Lugistricus chuanxiong
1 ¼ cups (300 ml) water

Preparation and use: Bring all ingredients to a quick boil, simmer for 20 minutes to reduce the volume to about half, and sip slowly while still warm. Using the same method, add more water in the evening and prepare the same tea. Discard the ingredients. The Chinese tonic Bei Qi Nao Zao Jiu supports the action of light tea. Take 2 teaspoons every morning and afternoon for 3 months. This is the most effective way to treat depression with herbs.

Note to this recipe: Anyone suffering from frequent depression must consult a physician. The herbal therapies suggested here can support medical treatment, but they cannot replace it. Chinese medicine too has very effective therapies against depression.

JAPAN
GREEN TEA AND ZEN CULTURE

Traditional Japanese medicine is thriving in contemporary Japan. It was developed many centuries ago out of the Chinese medical tradition. It is called *Kanpo*, "the Chinese method."

It is said that fifteen hundred years ago Korean physicians were summoned to the court of Japan to teach Chinese medicine. In AD 562 the Chinese doctor Zhi Cong brought acupuncture and moxibustion to Japan from the kingdom of Wu. The systematic study of Chinese medical knowledge, however, didn't begin in Japan until the year 623, when two Japanese monks, Enichi and Fukuin, returned to their homeland from China, where they had been studying medicine for fifteen years. They started Japan's first school of Chinese medicine.

During the subsequent centuries the Japanese version of Chinese medicine developed along its own lines, in part because it was forced to do so. The need for certain herbs that grow only in China made Japanese physicians look for native substitutes and also encouraged practitioners to incorporate many methods from their own native medical tradition. In this way the Chinese tradition accommodated itself to the needs and the lifestyle of the Japanese.

European Influence

In the sixteenth and seventeenth centuries, by which time *Kanpo* was well developed and established, some Spanish missionaries were allowed into Japan. These "southern barbarians" (*nanbanjin*) introduced their own religion and at the same time influenced Japanese medicine. Until that time, *Kanpo*, medical treatment by trained practitioners, had been available only to the aristocracy and the very wealthy. The Western monks, however, treated people of all walks of life with their "cosmopolitan medicine," as it was called. This turned out to be the most significant contribution of the West to Japan at that period. Today, that cosmopolitan medicine is the official and dominant form in Japan, supported by the state. Nonetheless, *Kanpo* has been able to hold its own as the primary alternative healing system.

Kanpo Specialties

In contrast to the often spectacularly quick results obtained by Western medicine, the gentle power of *Kanpo* is visible only in cases where the body's ability to heal itself has failed and health is declining. Among the well-developed techniques of *Kanpo* is a manual means of diagnosis and simultaneous treatment of illness. Japanese doctors base their work on the premise that palpitation of various areas of the abdomen reveals the pathology of different organs and at the same time permits their treatment. When an abdominal zone feels weak, it is assumed that the organ connected with that area is traumatized.

In the West, the best-known Japanese treatment technique is shiatsu, a special form of acupressure. Shiatsu is holistic, gentle and relaxing but also extremely effective. It aims at releasing energy blocks and achieving a harmonious flow of energy through the meridians. The shiatsu practitioner puts pressure on muscles and tendons, thus stimulating meridian points, and is thereby able to reach certain organs along those meridians. For example, headaches can be alleviated by pressure on the *Yin Tan* point between the eyebrows and by treatment of the organs of digestion, which are considered to be responsible for headaches.

Kanpo's use of herbs is distinctly different from Chinese herbal medicine. Japanese herbalists place greater emphasis on the purity of the ingredients, and they have developed their own recipes. In contrast to traditional Chinese medicine, which often prescribes extremely high dosages, *Kanpo* has deliberately aimed at keeping dosage to the minimum required. This has worked well. The number of herbal components, minerals and animal parts used is small compared with the Chinese pharmacopoeia; modern *Kanpo* physicians use only about 150 different substances. Moreover, all recipes are prepared for individual patients. Often effective only in combination with other prescribed methods of treatment, they are never meant for anyone else. Furthermore, prescriptions are continually adjusted as the patient's treatment progresses.

Another development of *Kanpo* is macrobiotics. This school of nutrition classifies all foods as Yin or Yang and aims to provide a balance of nutrients to the body. The macrobiotic "pyramid" prescribes that 50 percent of nourishment should consist of grains, 25 percent of fruit, 10 percent of plant and animal protein, and the remaining 15 percent of soy products and various beverages.

Many of today's Japanese doctors believe that parts of Western medicine can be usefully integrated into *Kanpo*, and vice versa. In an effort to bridge the gap between East and West, Japanese doctors often take training in both disciplines and allow the full range of their knowledge to enter into their study and evaluation of symptoms. When the word *Kanpo* is used with reference to herbal remedies, it always implies the application of the entire body of traditional Japanese medical knowledge.

Japanese Healing Herbs from Traditional Kanpo Medicine

Most of the healing herbs used in Japan grow exclusively in that country, though some also thrive in other parts of the Far East and in Europe. Because of Japanese medicine's Chinese roots, its use of familiar herbs may be different than in the West.

Daikon (Radish)

Raphanus sativus Daikon means "long root" and refers to the long white radish. Grated fresh radish is an excellent digestive. Japanese restaurants traditionally serve radish with sushi, to prevent protein oversaturation or oversatiation. After meals a teaspoon of fresh ground radish with a few drops of tamarind sauce does the trick.

Kuzu

Puerarua lobata/hirsuta Kuzu is a vine that grows wild in Japan. A starchy substance obtained from its root has been used both for healing and in cooking since the thirteenth century. Powdered *kuzu* is snow white in color and claylike in texture. To produce it the hard root has to be sawed, chopped and ground. Many Japanese remedies for intestinal weakness and digestive problems, as well as exhaustion and flu, will contain *kuzu*.

Kuzu is alkaline and contains many vitamins and minerals, and therefore has a very positive influence on the entire digestive system. Sour burping and heartburn, for example, can be cured quickly with *kuzu* cooked briefly in water. Dissolve one tablespoon *kuzu* powder in a little cold water and bring it to a boil after adding 200 ml water; stir steadily. When it boils, *kuzu* thickens and turns translucent. A few drops of soy sauce will give this tasteless mush some life.

Kuzu is available in health food stores and in some Oriental grocery stores.

Lotus Root

Nelumbrium nuciferum The root of the lotus plant is also used in cooking as well as for healing. In Japanese cuisine the root is appreciated for its decorative cross-section; it is often included in vegetable dishes. In *Kanpo* medicine lotus root is used against mucus collected in the respiratory system, as in coughs, bronchitis and asthma, and against sinusitis. One way to use it is to slice fresh lotus root or to soak dried lotus root slices. The root is then cooked for about 20 minutes, some tamarind-soy sauce is added and the dish is simmered for ten minutes more. The soup is then ready to drink. Japanese groceries offer lotus root frozen, dried, powdered and in cans.

Peach

Prunus persica In Japan the peach, or *momo*, is not just a fruit to be enjoyed; it is also a healing plant. The leaves of the peach tree yield a soothing jelly, which can strengthen a damaged intestinal tract. Although peach leaves are prescribed for gastritis, they can also be used against bronchitis and cough. The leaves contain a cyanogenous glycoside that calms and reduces irritation. As a secondary benefit it promotes urination and elimination, and reduces nausea.

Shiso

Perilla frutescens Shiso, which means "purple leaf," is a plant of the mint family. The *perilla* plant grows very quickly. Its purple leaves are used in the preservation of the famous

Umeboshi plum, for no other reason than that the aldehyde in *perilla* is a much more effective preservative than any synthetic substance. *Shiso* leaves also contain chlorophyll, vitamins, calcium, iron and phosphorus. In Japanese medicine the leaves are used in various combinations to calm the nervous system, to build up urine, to induce sweating, and with weak digestions, colds and coughs. The leaves preserved with the *Umeboshi* plums can be made into an effective remedy against food poisoning induced by eating bad fish. Soak the leaves in water and boil up into a tea.

The Tea Shrub

Camellia sinensis Tea is known the world over as a stimulating beverage. Its significance as a healing herb, however, is scarcely appreciated. The tea plant, *Camellia sinensis*, is used in healing as an astringent, to loosen mucus and to stimulate digestion.

There are three ways of treating the leaves of the tea shrub. Fermenting them completely produces black tea. Partial fermentation will result in yellow, or oolong, tea. Unfermented, or green, tea leaves retain most of their healing properties and are, therefore, the most highly valued by practitioners. Japan produces only green tea.

Green tea contains, in addition to caffeine and plenty of fluoride (which reduces cavities), a host of valuable catechins. These antioxidants are capable of combining with and disabling the free radicals that are said to play a role in the development of cancer and arteriosclerosis.

Advice: All brands of tea are likely to be heavily treated with pesticides. It is a good idea, especially if you consume a lot of tea, to buy organic brands whenever possible.

Ume

Prunus ume The *ume* tree is a relative of our apricot. This variety of apricot has special significance for the Japanese. The green fruit, inedible in its unripe condition, is processed into a wide range of products with remarkable healing properties. Best known is umeboshi, dried *ume* laid away in barrels with sea salt and *shiso* leaves for months or even years. In Japan, Korea, and China, *umeboshi* is prized as a universal healing agent and is also eaten as food. Some of the conditions treated with *umeboshi* are: food poisoning, edema, diarrhea, constipation, too much or too little stomach acid, travel sickness and headaches, fatigue, acid blood, liver problems and geriatric illnesses. *Ume* is also used to heighten vitality. What has been scientifically proven is the plant's efficacy as an antibacterial agent against such bacterial heavyweights as dysentery, staphylococcus and tuberculosis. It has also been shown that, against stomach or intestinal attacks or suspected food poisoning, *umeboshi* can be a quick remedy: just soak one dried fruit in *bancha* tea and eat it.

WONDERFUL TEA SPECIALTIES FROM THE LAND OF THE RISING SUN

Travel Tea

Travel tea is universally enjoyed in Japan and can be valuable for anyone living in the West too. In summer, travel tea is drunk because it will regulate body temperature. It is, however, also a genuine healing agent. Anyone who is ill can derive comfort from it, but for those suffering from slow digestion, diarrhea and headaches, it is particularly beneficial.

These are the proportions for the mixture:
11 parts water
1 part rice
1 pinch sea salt
a few drops tamari

Preparation and use: Roast the washed rice in a pan without fat, stirring constantly, until it is golden yellow. Measure 11 parts water to 1 part rice, bring to a boil and let simmer, uncovered, over a low flame for about 20 minutes. Add a pinch sea salt. Now pour through a cotton cloth, wrap the rice tight and strain out all the liquid. Add 1 or 2 drops of tamari to each cup, to give it more taste.

Mugisha, Roasted Barley Tea

Mugisha, or barley tea, is another of those classic hot beverages that refresh during the heat of summer. It can also counteract a surfeit of animal proteins and fats. It is possible to substitute wheat for the barley.

10 parts water
1 part barley or wheat kernels

Preparation and use: As for the rice tea above, the grain is dry-roasted until it colors (about 10 minutes), and then is brought to a quick boil and simmered for about 15 minutes. As a refreshment, *mugisha* can also be taken cold.

Shiitake Tea

The shiitake mushroom grows on oak. It is a very tasty mushroom that serves both as a food item and as a healing substance in Japan and can be found in good markets on this continent.

The tea prepared from this valuable fungus helps people whose Yang energy is too strong, particularly those with high blood pressure or high levels of blood cholesterol. It is also a good beverage to balance an excessively salty meal. Low energy people, whose kidneys tend to be sluggish, enjoy this tea a lot, and it also helps stressed nerves to relax.

1 shiitake mushroom
2 cups (500 ml) water
a pinch a sea salt

Preparation and use: Quarter the mushroom and bring it to a boil with the water and sea salt. Simmer it slowly until the volume of liquid is reduced to half. Drink only half of this tea immediately, keeping the rest for later the same day.

Note to this recipe: Shiitake tea is not meant for delicate people whose Yin energy is very pronounced, those who frequently shiver and whose hands and feet are often cold. This tea is Yin and would just make them worse. Robust Yang types, however, will experience this tea as comforting and balancing.

Mu Tea

Mu tea is a specialty of macrobiotics. It is revitalizing and regenerative. George Oshawa, the founder of this school of nutrition, composed this tea originally from sixteen ingredients, some as exotic as root of Japanese peony, sea nettle, bitter thistle, licorice root, ginger root and Chinese digitalis. Since these ingredients are generally unavailable in the West, there now exist some packaged Mu teas based on Dr. Oshawa's model, most of them with far fewer ingredients.

1 bag Mu tea
3 cups (700 ml) water

Preparation and use: People who are healthy but tired should open the tea bag and cook the contents for about 12 minutes in 3 cups of water. Those with digestive problems, a cough or menstrual cramps should increase the cooking time to 30 minutes, until half the liquid has boiled away. This is the appropriate daily dose.

Radish Tea

This is a very strong recipe, not suitable for children or for weak, delicate constitutions. Healthy, robust people, however, can really profit from radish tea when they run a fever due to a cold or when they have eaten foods that do not agree with them. The radish is guaranteed to bring the body into a sweat and thus to lower body temperature. Japanese people also drink this tea when they contract meat, fish or seafood poisoning.

2–3 tbsp. freshly grated radish or daikon
¼ tsp. freshly grated ginger

1 tsp. soy sauce
3 cups (700 ml) hot bancha *tea*

Preparation and use: Mix the radish with the ginger and soy sauce and pour the *bancha* tea over it. Mix well and drink it quickly, preferably all at once. Go to bed and cover yourself with a warm blanket. Radish tea should not be drunk more than once a day.

Lotus Root Tea

Fresh lotus root is best for this tea, but if it is not available, frozen, dried or powdered lotus root can be used. This is a very old Japanese remedy for mucus obstruction of the respiratory system, be it a cough, bronchitis or sinusitis. Even in cases of whooping cough, lotus tea has been found to be helpful. Lactating mothers will drink this tea if their baby has whooping cough in order to administer to their child the healing lotus root by way of their own milk.

0.4 oz. (10 g) dried lotus root
0.04 oz. (1 g) ginger powder
a pinch of sea salt
a few drops soy sauce

Preparation and use: Simmer the lotus root in 1 cup (250 ml) water for about 13 minutes, add the ginger and salt, and drink the tea when it is cool enough.

Black Bean Tea

Anyone who eats too many sweets and not enough fiber will have occasional digestive problems. When these arise, try this tea made of black soybeans.

1 tbsp. black soybeans
7 cups (2 l) water
a few drops of soy sauce

Preparation and use: Wash the beans and bring them to a boil in 7 cups (2 l) water. Simmer them slowly until the water is reduced by half. Strain and add some soy sauce. For an acutely slow gut, 3 cups a day can be taken. This tea is also supposed to calm overstressed nerves.

Variations on Kuzu Tea

Kuzu tea has a jellylike texture because it is made of starch. It has helped millions who suffer from heartburn, sour burping and other stomach problems. Even in cases of headache and feverish colds, *kuzu* tea will solve the problem via the digestive tract.

1 tsp. kuzu *powder*
1 large cup of water
soy sauce

Preparation and use: Dissolve the *kuzu* powder in 2 tablespoons of cold water and dilute with a cup of boiling water, stirring constantly. As the *kuzu* comes to a boil, it will thicken and take on a glassy translucency. You can improve the taste with some soy sauce.

Notes to this recipe: Many variations on this basic *kuzu* recipe are known to *Kanpo* medicine. Instead of using a whole cup of water, you can substitute for half of it the freshly pressed juice of an apple. This will stimulate the appetite or calm fidgeting. *Umbeshi kuzu* tea is made by mashing the flesh of an *umbeshi* and adding it to the *kuzu* that was mixed with cold water. This mixture is brought to a boil with 2 cups of water, after adding a few drops of fresh ginger juice. Add a bit of soy sauce when the mixture becomes translucent and eat this tea soup immediately. This particular *kuzu* recipe is very tasty. It raises energy levels and counteracts feelings of weakness. It will also be effective as a remedy against stomach and intestinal problems. A sufferer from diarrhea can safely eat 2 or 3 cups a day.

The Kombucha Mushroom Tea

Kombucha tea is a fermented drink based on a recipe two thousand years old. It is becoming

quite popular in Europe and North America. The Asian Kombucha mushroom, which is the source of the tea, is a traditional Far Eastern remedy against all sorts of metabolic complaints. Kombucha tea is refreshing, its taste being reminiscent of cider. It can be started with black, green, maté or herbal tea combined with sugar. During the process of fermentation, which takes about ten days, the mushroom adds many valuable nutrients to the developing tea, including important vitamins, minerals, enzymes, yeasts and even some caffeine.

The list of Kombucha's healing powers is impressive. The tea mushroom detoxifies, eliminates waste products, activates the metabolism, revitalizes and sanitizes the intestinal flora, inhibits viruses and bacteria, and enhances the performance of mind and body. It is said that, used regularly, the tea mushroom not only prolongs life but bestows immortality!

For 1 Kombucha tea:
3 ½ cups (1 l) water
7–8 tbsp. sugar
1–2 tsp. black or green tea, or 2 tsp. herbal tea
1 perfect Kombucha mushroom with enough fermented tea for a starter
a piece of cotton cloth
a rubber band
a strainer
a funnel
a Pyrex cooking pot

Preparation and use: Heat the water in the Pyrex pot and add the sugar, stirring until it dissolves. Remove the pot from the heat and add the tea. Let the tea steep, covered, for 15 minutes. Strain the tea and let it cool to lukewarm.

Pour the liquid in which the mushroom is held into a glass container or bowl. Pour in the tea. The liquid should be at least 3 fingers deep. Put the mushroom in the liquid. Cover the top of the container with the cotton cloth and fasten it in place with the rubber band. The mushroom will now need to stand in a cool, well-ventilated place. It needs lots of fresh air, but it should also stay warm, although without direct sunshine. After 8 to 10 days the tea will be ready. Take out the mushroom and rinse it well under running water. Set it aside for the moment, with enough of your tea to start again. Strain your Kombucha tea into a pitcher and store it in the refrigerator. After the glass container has been thoroughly washed with hot water, a new fermentation process can begin.

Do not drink too much of your tea! A small glass (½ cup or ⅛ l) first thing in the morning, one after lunch and perhaps another small glass before going to bed will suffice. Children should not drink more than 1 cup (¼ l) per day. As with any other natural therapy, one needs to take breaks with Kombucha as well. To regenerate intestinal flora or when chronically ill, take the tea for 6 months and then give yourself a 2-month break.

Notes to this recipe: It is possible to try out Kombucha before embarking on this rather complex process, by buying a package of Kombucha tea bags. They are sold in health food stores. There even exists a Kombucha extract for diabetics. Another interesting product is the liquid Kombucha of Dr. Sklenar. This essence contains high concentrations of all the active ingredients, and is convenient when traveling.

Green Tea: Japan's National Drink

The Japanese national beverage is also the most popular prepared drink in the world, namely tea, a healing agent as well as a pleasant refreshment. The Japanese will always prefer green tea to black. Green tea wakes you up and promotes concentration without making you jittery. It is the ideal nerve tonic for those who do mental work; it also serves those who meditate. Green tea drinking spread in Japan with the acceptance of Zen Buddhism, and it is still an important part of Zen ceremonies.

The Japanese Tea Ceremony

Chanoyu is the word used for the tea ceremony; it actually means "hot water for tea." The ritual of tea making expresses the philosophy of Tao. Hundreds of schools teach the tea ceremony in Japan today. To do it right, the tea ceremony requires years of training and practice, because what for Westerners is an insignificant, everyday action is ultimately carried out with complete attention, total awareness and great love for each detail. On a mat made of rice straw the participants kneel and prepare, serve and drink green tea. Their actions, however, have become a form of meditation. This means that each movement expresses gratitude; the objects are handled with perfect focus on what is being done at each moment. This merging with what is happening at the moment is the first principle of Zen Buddhism.

After the guests have seated themselves on the mat, the host sets out the utensils, which may include an incense burner. The picture on page 26 shows the serenity that is expressed even in the design of the utensils. The guests may take a short break to rinse their mouths outdoors and then five gong beats announce the beginning of the ceremony. The tea master now presents the clay tea bowl, which contains a bamboo whisk, a cloth and a teaspoon. Each action is exactly prescribed: how to fold the cloth, how to hold the tea ladle, how to open the tea jar, how to knock the tea off the teaspoon. The ingredients and procedures are also clearly defined. Pure water has to be boiled. Leaves of *Matcha* tea are to be worked into a powder using a stone mortar. The ground *Matcha* tea is then put into a bowl, using the bamboo spoon, the *cha-shaku*. The tea is brewed with water that has cooled down to 125 to 140 degrees Fahrenheit (50–60°C). The bamboo whisk, the *chasen*, serves to mix the powdered tea with the hot water. This is followed by the act of "putting together and allowing to unfold," pouring into bowls and serving the tea. This is done with deference, to express the host's respect for his guests. The tea is poured following certain traditional rules. After mutual bows, the guest accepts the tea bowl and places it on his or her left palm. The careful turning of the bowl before drinking also expresses the guest's deference and gratitude to the tea and to the host, and is as much part of the tea ceremony as the movements of the host. The whole ritual teaches us to offer respect, deference, gratitude and humility to all things—to human beings, to plants, to food, to the moment.

The Most Significant Green Tea Varieties of Japan

Matcha: These noble tea leaves grow in the shade. They are used in the tea ceremony. *Matsu* refers to the outermost tip of trees and leaves;

cha means "tea." For this tea, the leaves of the youngest twigs are picked. Shortly before sale or before serving, *Matcha* tea is ground to a powder in a stone mortar. The powder is placed in a tea bowl, covered with water that has boiled and then cooled to about 60 degrees, and whisked to a froth with a bamboo tool made for that purpose. (See The Japanese Tea Ceremony, page 34.)

Sencha: This is the most popular tea in Japan. The tea leaves are steamed for 30 seconds and then dried by a hot-air process. They end up looking like grass. *Sencha* tea is slightly bitter and has a golden yellow color. It comes in three different qualities: superior, medium and low.

Gyokuro: *Gyokuro* means "noble drops of dew." Here we are dealing with the best and most expensive tea available. The famous aroma of *Gyokuro* is only possible because it is harvested in May, when the young shoots first open, and only the most tender of tea leaves are used. To brew this strong, golden green tea, pour water that has cooled down to 60 degrees over the leaves in the cup.

Bancha: *Bancha* is the lowest-quality green tea. It is made from the older leaves of the tree, after the first harvest. Leaves from the first harvest are used to make *Ichi-nen Bancha*, those from the second harvest produce *Ni-nen Bancha*. Roasted *Bancha* is called *Honjicha*. *Gen-maicha* refers to *Bancha* tea mixes with one-half roasted whole rice kernels. All *Bancha* teas stimulate the digestion.

Kuchicha: Known in Japan as the worst tea, it is actually the healthiest. It contains the twigs of the tea shrub but none of its leaves. Its other name is twig tea. It contains hardly any caffeine, and thus is suitable even for children. It must simmer for 10 minutes in a pot. Twig tea can improve kidney and bladder complaints, neurasthenia and fatigue.

The Seven Rules for Preparing Green Tea

1. Warm the pot: Fill the teapot with hot water that you discard just before brewing the tea.
2. Dosage: Use one flat teaspoon per cup. When you make four or five cups, add an extra teaspoon of tea to the pot.
3. Water: Let the boiled water cool to 140 to 160 degrees Fahrenheit (60–70°C) before pouring it over the tea leaves.
   Note: Use water that is calcium-free if possible. The less calcium there is in the water, the more taste the tea will have.
4. Steeping: Lower-quality teas steep for only one minute, the better ones for a maximum of three minutes. Letting green tea steep for four to six minutes will make it taste stronger and slightly bitter, but it will reduce its stimulating effect.
5. Pouring: First, a little tea is poured into each cup. Then all the cups are filled.
6. Drinking: Connoisseurs will drink green tea straight. You can add a little sugar and a mint leaf.
7. Repeated steeping: The leaves in the pot can be steeped at least twice. The second and third times, however, the leaves are steeped only half as long as the first time.

It's Teatime—Unusual Recipes Using Green Tea

Green Iced Tea

A refreshing summer drink for young and old, East or West.

For 2 cups (½ l) tea:
2–3 tsp. of the green tea of your choice
¼ stick cinnamon
1 tsp. honey
½ tsp. lemon juice
a few drops Angostura Bitters
2 cups (½ l) water

Preparation and use: Steep the green tea with the cinnamon for about 3 minutes using water that has cooled down somewhat after boiling. Strain and add the honey, lemon juice and Angostura Bitters. Stir and let cool.

Green Tea Cookies

Should you ever want to serve something unusual with tea, cookies made with green tea are an ideal accompaniment because they agreeably complement the aroma of tea.

12 oz. (350 g) wheat flour
3 tsp. baking powder
1 tsp. salt
2 oz. (60 g) brown sugar
2 oz. (50 g) butter
2 eggs
3 oz. (100 ml) strong green tea
(made with about 0.1 oz./3 g green tea leaves)

Preparation and use: Stir or sift the flour with the baking powder, salt and 1 ½ oz. (50 g) of the sugar. Beat the eggs with the green tea, then make a smooth dough with the flour, the butter and most of the egg mixture. Roll the dough about ⁴⁄₁₀ inch (1 cm) thick and cut into pieces 2 ½ to 3 inches (6–8 cm) square. Fold the squares loosely into triangles. Place them on a cookie sheet lined with waxed paper and brush their tops with the remaining egg-tea mixture. Sprinkle with the remaining brown sugar. Place in an oven that is preheated to 350°F (180°C). Bake the cookies for about 25 minutes. Best served while still warm.

Tamari-*Bancha*

Tamari-*Bancha* is a variation on green tea that will strike Westerners as unusual, but it is particularly healthy. In this case green tea is combined with a salty taste. This tea is also called *sho-ban*; it is drunk in Japan as a general pick-me-up. Both ingredients of *sho-ban*, namely *bancha* tea and soy sauce, act to balance acidity of the blood, a condition that is very common in the West. *Sho-ban* is a blessing for people who frequently suffer from stomach acid and its usual ramifications. Even stomach ache and bloating are relieved by this tea.

1 cup (¼ l) hot bancha tea
1–2 teaspoons tamari sauce
Optional: *a pinch of ground ginger*

Preparation and use: Place the tamari soy sauce into a cup, pour the *bancha* tea over it and drink immediately. You can drink 2 cups a day, but after 4 days of this take a few days off. If you are trying to treat stomach or intestinal problems, it is best to include the ginger powder in the recipe.

INDIA
THE EXQUISITE REMEDIES OF AYURVEDA

The word *Ayurveda* is composed of two Sanskrit stems: *ayur*, which means "life," and *veda*, "knowledge." The knowledge of life: this is the basis of Indian folk medicine, which is about 2,500 years old. It is not surprising, then, that Ayurvedic medicine has as one of its aims to further the spiritual consciousness and the search for meaning in each patient's life. These things, as much as the maintenance of a healthy lifestyle, are considered the responsibility of every human being, and Ayurveda is there to enable the individual to unfold in the direction of physical, emotional and spiritual health. Illness is seen as imbalance. To restore equilibrium, the patient is treated on the physical, emotional and spiritual levels. While herbs and certain nutrients are used in Ayurveda, treatment always includes other modes, for example massage with fragrant oils and the use of strong, aromatic incense. Colors too are employed in healing, and physical movement and meditation are considered healing modalities in the context of a holistic view of health.

The Three *Doshas*

Ayurveda's view of mankind is encompassed by the typology of the three *doshas*, the primary factors of the human body: *vata*, *pitta* and *kapha*. *Vata* roughly corresponds to the melancholic type, *pitta* to the choleric type and *kapha* to the phlegmatic type. All three *doshas* are composed of the five natural elements: earth, water, fire, air and ether (space). Air and ether produce *vata* (wind), fire produces *pitta* (fire or bile), and earth and water produce *kapha* (phlegm). To demonstrate how this approach plays out in diagnosis and treatment, a condition that is caused by excess phlegm or mucus, say a cough or an edema, is treated with warm, light and dry nutrients or with a fast, and the patient is instructed to avoid cold liquids.

The Six Different Tastes

The taste of a healing herb or food plays an important role in Ayurveda. The six tastes are sweet, salty, sharp, tart, astringent and bitter. These tastes lead the body in the direction of one of the *doshas*, that is, increasing or decreasing them in relation to one another. Since one-sided nutrition will lead to imbalance in the *doshas* and to illness, it is important to balance the tastes in the foods one consumes. When imbalances occur, more substances of a certain taste need to be ingested, to restore the inner equilibrium.

The Classification of Nutrients by Taste

Among the many "sweet" foods we find yams, rice and cashews. This category is called *madhura* and is said to promote the formation of bodily fluids, including sperm and mother's milk. *Madhura* foods are most appropriate for certain *pitta* problems, such as the accumulation of poisons and waste in the body. People with *kapha* constitutions, however, tend to get colds and rheumatic pains and should avoid these foods as much as possible.

Tart foods, also called *amla*, such as lemons, spinach and moss berries (also called small cranberries), reduce *vata* and increase *kapha* and *pitta*. They will stimulate the digestion and give strength when needed.

Salty is called *lavana* in Ayurveda. Here we find mineral salts or seaweed. Such things increase *pitta* and *kapha*. Salt holds liquids in the body and combines with toxins. Salty foods are eaten to dissolve phlegm.

Among the sharp-tasting, or *katu*, foods we find horseradish, basil and cloves. They will heighten *vata* and *pitta* and lessen *kapha*. These substances stimulate and warm the system and are applied against colds, lethargy and depression.

The bitter taste is called *tikta*. Plants that are considered bitter are chicory, turmeric and artichokes. They increase *vata* and dampen *pitta* and *kapha*. They work by stimulating the digestion, absorbing phlegm and thereby freeing the body of "fire poisons." Foods of this category are effective with fever and skin diseases.

Astringent substances (*kasaya*) include sage, blueberries and dried strawberry leaves. They are light, cold and dry. They enhance *vata* and counteract *pitta* and *kapha*. These herbs are taken against diarrhea and excessive menstrual flow.

The Chakras

The science of the chakras is an important aspect of Ayurveda. The word *chakra* means "wheel or whirl of energy." Chakras are subtle energy centers that control all bodily functions, organs and glands. The human body contains seven main chakras. Ayurvedic medicine stimulates chakras either by direct external application of certain herbs or their essential oils to the chakra or by administering appropriate herbs internally.

Many Ayurvedic therapy modes are aimed at harmonizing the chakras: nutrition, massage, movement, deep relaxation, as well as color, chanting and ritualistic purification. Herbs that strengthen the immune system, such as *ashwa-gandha*, *shatavari* or *guduchi*, can also release the vitality of the chakra system. Here is a list of the chakras and of the organs and herbs associated with each:

- Crown chakra—Organ: pineal body; Herbs: *gotu kola*, nutmeg
- Brow chakra—Organ: pituitary gland Herbs: sandalwood, horse elder (*Inula Helenium*)
- Throat chakra—Organ: thyroid gland Herbs: clove, vervain
- Heart chakra—Organ: thymus gland Herbs: saffron, rose
- Solar plexus chakra—Organs: liver, adrenals Herbs: turmeric, lemon balm
- Sacral chakra—Organ: testicles, ovaries Herbs: coriander, fennel
- Root chakra—Organs: Uterus, prostate Herbs: *ashwagandha*, *haritaki*

When all the fast-whirling energy vortexes are functioning and aligned, the life energy unfolds perfectly throughout the body. This force, also called *ojas*, is associated in Western medicine with the immune system or the self-healing power of the body. When one of the chakras slows down, becomes displaced or even ceases to function, the energy flow is blocked and illness results. Aging and bodily decay are speeded up. Early signs of this condition can be something as innocuous as slight discomfort or fatigue.

The bounty of Indian spices in one glance: star anise, licorice, cardamom, allspice, black pepper, cloves, and more.

The Central Herbs and Spices of Ayurvedic Medicine

Ashwagandha

Withania omnifera *Ashwagandha* is a very important healing plant in Ayurvedic medicine. Indian doctors value it the way their Chinese counterparts esteem ginseng, but *ashwagandha* is a lot less expensive. As with ginseng, only the root is used, and it has similar virtues, namely, the power to build the immune system and general strengthening abilities. A well-known aphrodisiac and rejuvenating tonic, it is taken to combat exhaustion and general weakness.

Weak children, elderly men and people recovering from long illness will certainly benefit from the revitalizing powers of this plant, but it is also recommended for anyone who is stressed, overworked, nervous or unable to sleep.

Other conditions for which *ashwagandha* is prescribed include difficulty in concentrating, rheumatism, skin problems, anemia, atrophying muscles, back pain and even multiple sclerosis. *Ashwagandha* is usually taken as a milky decoction sweetened with honey, and this is the most effective way if you are trying to hold off the symptoms of aging or to energize your metabolism. The plant has a calming and freeing effect on the spirit.

One of *ashwagandha*'s major healing functions arises from its special affinity for the reproductive organs of both men and women. Women are given this natural tonic to enhance their receptivity during conception, and during pregnancy they take it to stabilize the embryo. Men rely on the plant's aphrodisiac powers and use it against infertility due to a low sperm count.

Fenugreek

Trigonella foenum-greacum Fenugreek is esteemed worldwide as among the oldest healing herbs. Ayurveda uses the leaves and the seeds of *methi*, as they call fenugreek. The leaves are dried, fried in clarified butter (ghee), ground and used as a spice. The seed is used as a tonic at times of weakness or stress and after illness. The shoots of fenugreek are very tasty; they alleviate digestive problems, liver ailments and fatigue.

Here is a simple recipe for shattered nerves: boil a teaspoon of fenugreek seeds in about a cup of milk, strain, sweeten with honey, and drink.

Ginger

Zingiber officinale The healing powers of ginger are legendary and are valued by medical traditions the world over. Ginger root has been used by both Indian and Chinese doctors for over two thousand years. Western medicine too has used ginger for healing. The plant's original habitat was in East Asia, but today it is cultivated in many tropical regions, including the West Indies and Hawaii. Because of its hot and dry qualities, ginger is used everywhere to heat the stomach and as a cold remedy. Other benefits of ginger include stimulating circulation, relaxing the peripheral blood vessels, aiding perspiration, loosening phlegm and cramps, alleviating bloating and acting as an antiseptic. Western medicine has been using ginger for some decades against nausea, including morning sickness and travel sickness. Capsules of dried, ground ginger can be taken for this purpose. Ginger is used in Chinese medicine to counteract the poisons in some other healing herbs.

Cardamom

Elettaria cardamomum The queen of spices, cardamom, grows in Sri Lanka, Burma and India. In Ayurvedic cooking, cardamom is usually combined with cloves, ginger, turmeric and cinnamon. This combination of tastes is found in many Ayurvedic teas. The marvelous fragrance of cardamom, which reminds us of Christmas cookies, bestows mental clarity and joy; as a spice it stimulates primarily the stomach, alleviates bloating and lack of appetite, and strengthens the heart. Chewing a pod of cardamom after a meal will promote its digestion and, as a bonus, freshen the breath. Ayurvedic medicine also uses cardamom capsules in healing congestion of the bronchial tubes and sinuses. In Arab countries and in India, coffee and black tea are prepared with cardamom, in order to lessen the side effects of the caffeine and to lend the brew an aromatic appeal.

Long Pepper

Piper longum Called *pipali* in Sanskrit, this plant originated in southern India and Sri Lanka. The aroma of *pipali* resembles that of ginger. Ayurvedic cooking uses long pepper in vegetable dishes, chutneys and cooling salads, such as cucumber salad. As a healing agent, *pipali* stimulates digestion and reduces *ama*, the harmful wastes that accumulate in the body. It is also employed by Ayurvedic doctors to balance *kapha* and *vata* and to loosen mucus in cases of bronchitis.

Almonds

Amygdali amarae semen and ***A. dulcis semen*** As the botanical names imply, there is a distinction between sweet and bitter almonds.

The almond tree (*Amygdalus communis*) grows in India, and almonds are as indispensable to Ayurvedic cuisine as they are to our own. The sweet variety is a classic ingredient in sweets and baked goods, but it is also used to give crunch to salads and vegetable dishes. Only bitter almonds are used as a spice, and the prussic acid contained in bitter almond oil makes it a substance to be used with great care. Medically speaking, however, almonds are an excellent nerve tonic. Ayurvedic doctors use almonds to calm *vata* and to increase psychic endurance. Almond oil is good to use in massages intended to strengthen the nerves.

Cloves

Syzygium aromaticum/Eugenia caryophyllata Cloves were regarded as a wonder drug in the Middle Ages, when spices imported from far regions were as precious as gold. Cloves are the hand-picked buds of the clove tree, which originally grew in the Molucca Islands but was long ago introduced into China and India. Today, this ten-meter-high evergreen is cultivated in many tropical countries. Cloves are used in cooking by many traditions around the globe because of their sweet aroma and fiery-spicy taste. They are variously combined with caraway, cardamom, paprika and ginger. Essential oil of clove is of particular interest. It contains eugenol, a strongly antiseptic and analgesic substance, which is used in dentistry.

Black Pepper

Piper nigrum The first written reference to black pepper in India, its native country, goes back three thousand years, to the Vedas. Its original habitat was the steamy forests of southern

Asia and it is still grown mostly in India, Sri Lanka, other parts of Southeast Asia, and Brazil. The evergreen vine often climbs to a height of nine meters. From the flower develops the single seed, which is known the world over, whole, crushed, ground rough or fine. It is used both in cooking and in medicine. The fiery effect of black pepper stimulates digestion. Ayurvedic medicine uses black pepper with ginger and long pepper. This fiery trio bears the name *trikatu*, triple sharpness.

Mustard Seeds

Semen sinapis alba and nigrae Mustard seeds can be white or black; both types are used as spices and to prepare mustard paste. Whole mustard seeds are often added to pickles, for example. Mustard seeds are marketed mostly in ground form or as prepared mustards. Mustard is also used in many foods that stimulate the appetite, often combined with vinegar, but also in various sausages and other meat products. Black mustard is hotter than white. In healing, both types of mustard are used. They are skin irritants and generate beneficial surface heat if rubbed on body parts affected by rheumatic diseases.

Shatavari

Asparagus racemosus For women, *shatavari* is one of the most important rejuvenating herbs in all of Ayurveda. The root of the plant is cooked in milk, along with ghee, cane sugar and honey. The root's effect on the female sex organs is pronounced: it is calming while also strengthening, it stimulates urine and milk production, and it dissolves phlegm.

For many centuries *shatavari* has been used for all female complaints, ranging from low libido through infertility and hormonal disturbances to insufficient milk flow. During menopause the plant is also useful because it contains many substances that stimulate normal hormone production. The name alone, which means "she who has a hundred men," suggests the affinity of the plant for the lower abdominal region.

Men react to this Indian love root by producing more semen. *Shatavari* is also used in cases of gastritis and stomach ulcers, excessive stomach acidity, diarrhea and dysentery. Irritated mucus membranes in the urinary or respiratory system also respond well to the healing components of *shatavari*. Moreover, because the plant is nutritious and expels toxins, it is used in the treatment of fevers and is among the foods served to convalescents.

THE MOST TASTY TEA RECIPES OF AYURVEDA

Flower Power Yogi Tea

This tea was created according to the ancient principles of Ayurvedic medicine, but it was first made in California during the 1960s. Its creator was Yogi Bhajan, an Indian spiritual instructor, who was teaching yoga at the University of California during that period. Yogi Bhajan made this tea expressly for the many American flower children who were inspired by Indian culture to study yoga. At the beginning the tea was drunk mostly in the yoga centers that were shooting up like mushrooms. Since many of the flower children of the sixties and seventies were experimenting with drugs, the tea takes this fact into account: in addition to being a tonic, it has a strong antitoxic effect.

Since those days yogi tea has become a well-known commercial brand, available in any health food store and many good supermarkets. But one can still make it from scratch.

For one cup:
seeds from 4 green cardamom pods
4 whole black peppercorns
3 whole cloves
½ cinnamon stick
1 slice ginger
1 pinch black tea
1 ¼ cups (280 ml) water
some milk

Preparation and use: Mash the spices in a stone mortar and place them in a pot. Add the water and simmer for 20 minutes. Add a pinch of black tea and some milk and bring to a brief boil. Sweeten with some honey or cane sugar. This original recipe is not only tasty, but it strengthens the nerves and lifts the spirit, while still keeping your feet on the ground. Drink this tea when you feel tired or depressed, or when you feel a cold coming on. Overall, yogi tea boosts your energy and strengthens your resistance. It is a good winter tea.

Note to this recipe: In old India, yogi tea meant something slightly different. It was a spice tea, in which black tea leaves had no part. Yogi Bhajan's addition of a pinch of black tea counteracts with its cooling tendencies the heating effect of the spices. Black pepper purifies the blood, cardamom revs up the digestion and the milk cuts the sharpness of the spices.

In medieval Europe, before electricity arrived to heat and light the cold, dark winter months, the fiery spices of the East were sought-after remedies for the prevailing winter blues. In the cold climate of middle Europe it was common knowledge that the spices, which had ripened under the hot tropical sun, could lighten the spirit. It is not for nothing that spices were weighed against pure gold! The main reason Christopher Columbus started on his daring journey was to find another route to India, for the cheaper import of spices to Europe. So it is by no means an accident that many traditional gingerbread recipes contain the exact same spices as this yogi tea. After all, gingerbread is a seasonal food, served around Christmas, at the darkest time of the bitter European winter.

Golden Milk

This golden yellow milk drink is a true blessing to all who practice hatha yoga. The stretches in the exercises can produce sore joints, to the point where many a practitioner has had to give up his beloved yoga classes, but Golden Milk has helped many to continue.

For 2 cups (½ l) of the beverage:
1 tbsp. turmeric powder
2 cups (½ l) milk
1 cup (¼ l) water

Preparation and use: Simmer the turmeric for 8 minutes over low heat in the water.
Warning: During this process a thick yellow paste may result, which burns very easily. Do not leave the stove while the turmeric is simmering, but stir it constantly with a whisk and keep the heat low. Add the milk and bring to a quick boil. Sweeten with honey or cane sugar. Drink Golden Milk on days when you are doing yoga exercises. Even when you experience no pain, this is an excellent insurance policy for the joints.
Note to this recipe: Golden Milk does wonders with all ailments arising from overworked joints. Professional ballet dancers, athletes and acrobats have found it a very useful friend. The turmeric is predigested by being boiled and in this form can easily be absorbed by the body.

Ginger Tea for Women

This ginger tea is extraordinarily healing for all female organs and the intestines, as well as for stressed nerves and a sluggish metabolism.

a thumb-sized piece of ginger
2 cups (½ l) milk
1 cups (¼ l) water

Preparation and use: Peel the ginger and grate or slice very fine. Simmer very slowly for about 20 minutes in the water. Now add up to 2 cups (½ l) milk and let it boil up. Remove from the heat and sweeten with honey or cane sugar. Ginger tea is best consumed in small sips over the course of the day, as required. In the morning and before meals it stimulates digestion; on cold winter afternoons it warms and protects from the flu. Many women take the tea after miscarriages or abdominal surgery, to promote the healing of the uterus.
Note to this recipe: Ginger tea is so effective against ailments of the reproductive and digestive systems because it stimulates circulation and supports a good blood supply to these organs. Bloating can be treated with this tea, by adding a pinch of cinnamon. In the presence of stomach ulcers, however, modest amounts of this tea are recommended and the quantity of ginger can be cut down. Similarly, in the early weeks of pregnancy, the further stimulation of blood flow into the abdomen is not recommended, so go easy on ginger at this time. Modest amounts, however, are a great remedy for morning sickness.

Jalaa Jeera

Jalaa Jeera is a very effective Ayurvedic weight-loss tea. The combination of ingredients not only reduces excess body fat; it also exerts a very strong cleansing effect on the organism. In contrast to many Chinese slimming teas, *Jalaa Jeera* contains no senna fruit or leaves and does not have the same laxative action. Nonetheless, the tea's chemical components do cleanse the lining of the intestines and invigorate their functioning. Therefore, the complexion clears up with the therapeutic use of this tea. It also happens to be high in vitamin C.

For 6 cups (1 ½ l) tea:
½–¾ cups (125–190 ml) fresh or
dried mint leaves
1 lb. (450 g) cumin seed
1 oz. (30 g) fresh or frozen tamarind
½ tsp. rock salt
8 organic lemons
1 tsp. freshly ground black pepper
6 cups (1 ½ l) water

Preparation and use: Quarter the lemons and bring them to a boil with all other ingredients. Allow the ingredients to simmer over the lowest possible heat for 4 or 5 hours. The long cooking time is needed to extract the essence of the cumin seeds. Strain but do not throw out the tea ingredients, as they can be brewed again several times, except for the lemons, which will have to be replaced each time. You can drink *Jalaa Jeera* hot or cold. It can be stored in the refrigerator for about a week. To lose weight you have to drink 2 or 3 cups during the course of the day. The tea combines well with a weight-loss diet.

Potency Potion for Men

In India this is a well-known potency potion, a drink that balances sexual energy and relieves impotence. This tasty milk drink will, however, benefit the entire male nervous system.

For 1 cup (250 ml):
6 peeled almonds
3 crushed cardamom seeds
½ tsp. honey
1 cup (250 ml) milk

Preparation and use: Place all ingredients into a blender and mix till the drink is completely creamy. So that the active ingredients are fully absorbed by the body, no food should be eaten for 4 hours after the potency drink. Take a cup of the potion as needed.

Carob Delight

The "delights" of Ayurvedic cuisine are tasty treasures that simultaneously gratify, nourish, strengthen and heal the human body. The taste of this carob delight is as carefully balanced as its ingredients. This delicious drink is bound to please children and adults.

For 3–4 people:
9–10 whole green cardamom pods
2 cups (500 ml) water
2 ½ cups (625 ml) milk
¼ cup (60 ml) carob powder
honey or cane sugar

Preparation and use: Crush the cardamom pods in a mortar and simmer in the water for 10 minutes. Pour about a quarter of the water into a mixing bowl with the carob powder and beat with a whisk. Add the rest of the water, then the milk, stir very well and return to the pot. Bring the delight to a boil, let it cool and strain it. Sweeten it with honey or cane sugar.

Note to this recipe: This recipe comes from the tradition of the Golden Temple Meals. The Golden Temple, the holiest site of the Sikhs, is located in Amritsar in the Punjab. Traditionally, at the gates of the temple, a *langar*, a free feast, is served to the poor. About ten thousand meals are served there every day. Inspired by the wave of Indian lore that flooded Europe and the United States in the seventies and eighties, several Golden Temple restaurants were opened on both continents. Using the recipes of the *langar*, these places serve food and beverages to the poor.

Ayurveda *Rash* Tea

This *rash* is a very special spice and mountain-herb tea from the Nepalese part of the Himalayas. The natives there drink it for warmth and strength in the cold months. Its list of ingredients includes, for example, sugar grass or sorgo (*Polinia cumingii*), the bark of the Himalayan cedar and of the cinnamon tree, cloves, cardamom, mallow, rose moss flowers (*Portulaca grandiflora*) and white basil. The mixture is available for sale in Europe but is not yet available in North America.

2 cups (½ l) water
2 cups (½ l) milk
1 tsp. Ayurveda rash

Preparation and use: Bring the water and milk to a boil and add the *rash*. Allow to simmer

very gently for 5 to 10 minutes, then strain. Sweeten the tea if you like, with honey or cane sugar. Drink this tea in the winter, maybe after a long walk.

Date Milk

This nutritious and uplifting tonic tea is appreciated in Arab countries as well as India. It is said that dates preserve youth.

6 fresh dates
1 cup (250 ml) milk

Preparation and use: Halve the dates and remove the pits. Let them simmer in the milk over low heat for about 20 minutes, then strain. Drink a cup of this tea as you need it.

TIBET
HEALING POWER AND PHILOSOPHY FROM THE ROOF OF THE WORLD

Tibetan medicine is one of the oldest holistic medical systems in the world. For some years now we have seen a growing Western fascination with the wisdom that was being discovered among these snow-covered peaks. Buddhists everywhere and many North American and European physicians, botanists and pharmacologists are taking seriously the knowledge distilled over the centuries in this magical region.

We have the Dalai Lama to thank for the fact that the old knowledge of the Tibetan people has not been completely eradicated. When the Chinese People's Liberation Army invaded Tibet under Mao Tse-tung, they destroyed books and documents that had been collected over millennia in the monastic universities. The fourteenth Dalai Lama, whom his people venerate as the religious and political head of their state, fled into exile. He settled in the north Indian state of Dharamsala. Along with their leader, about ninety thousand Tibetans fled their country and went to live in India or Nepal. In this way much of Tibetan medical knowledge was preserved and opened to the rest of the world. Only two years after his flight over the mountains, the Dalai Lama founded the Tibetan Medical and Astrological Institute in Dharamsala. *Men-tsee-Khang*, as the school of Tibetan medicine is called, today encompasses a hospital, a mobile clinic, a pharmacy and a factory where Tibetan healing products are made according to the old formulas. Moreover, the institute has branches all over India and Nepal. There are several branches in North America which house a resident physician and a pharmacy.

Even in Chinese-occupied Tibet itself there has been a new opening to the old wisdom of the country. In the last few years the Chinese have recognized the efficacy of Tibetan medical methods. The authorities permitted Professor Khenpo Troru Tsenam to restore one of the few intact medical institutes, the Astro-Medical Institute in Lhasa, Tibet. He is one of the leading scholars of Tibetan medicine. The institute, *Mentsikhang*, is in full flower and includes a large teaching hospital and a factory making healing products. The Chinese do oversee the curriculum, however, and have placed many restrictions on academic freedom.

Ancient Tibetan medicine is also being adjusted to the requirements of our times. If this is accomplished in an intelligent manner, it is due to the foresight of Buddhist monk physicians like Troru Tsenam and Tensin Choedrak. The production of healing teas and herbal capsules is no longer restricted to the great healing centers in India and Tibet, either. In Switzerland, where many Tibetans have settled, the manufacture of standardized Tibetan herbal remedies has been successfully carried out for many years. However, North America still imports most of its standardized Tibetan herbal remedies from the Orient and Europe, rather than manufacture them domestically.

Buddhist Religion and Healing Arts

The present form of Tibetan medicine began in the seventh century AD. At that time the thirty-second Tibetan king, Song Tsen Gampo (617–49), married two princesses. One was Chinese; her name was Wencheng. The other was Nepalese; she was called Bhrikuti. Both were followers of

The gathering of healing plants is a religious act for Tibetans. Here we see the ingredients used to make Tibetan Butter Tea.

the Buddha, and between them they converted their king. Buddhist monks soon brought their holistic medicine to Tibet. Buddhist thought began replacing *Bön*, the ancient native shamanistic beliefs and medical lore of Tibet.

King Tsen Gampo supported the new trend in medicine, encouraging new ideas. The world's first international medical congress was held during his reign. Doctors and scholars were invited from India, China, Mongolia, Nepal, Turkestan, Persia and even distant Greece. In time, Tibetan physicians developed a synthesis of therapeutic methods culled from the Ayurvedic traditions of India, the ancient medical knowledge of China and the Unani system of Persia. Over time all this knowledge was melded into an independent holistic system of healing—the Tibetan medicine we know today.

Just as in medieval Europe the monasteries maintained and developed the arts of healing, so in Tibet the Buddhist monasteries were the great centers of learning. At the monasteries the monks studied not just religion but medicine, and they practiced it as well. Of course we have found out that Tibetan medicine works even when neither physician nor patient is Buddhist.

Since the seventeenth century, the form and content of Tibetan medicine have changed very little. The fifth Dalai Lama (1617–82) was a great supporter of medical knowledge. In his time *The 79-Picture Scroll* was created, which recorded once and for all the entire body of Tibetan medical teachings. To this day these detailed medical pictures play an important part in the training of Tibetan physicians.

The Three Poisons of the Mind

Tibetan medicine identifies the cause of all suffering in the three poisons of the mind. Greed (or attachment) encompasses the range of human emotions from desire to jealous sexual passion. Hate, anger or aggression includes all shades from mild frustration to burning hatred. The third poison, blindness or closed-mindedness, ranges from mental dullness to egomania; it is a lack of recognition of the innate purity of the spirit.

The three mental poisons are reflected in the body, in the form of the three "bodily fluids" or humors: wind (*loong*), bile (*tripa*) and phlegm (*begen*). The teaching about the three humors forms the basis of Tibetan medicine. On many levels the "humors" have a purely symbolic meaning. They are also seen as the "three principles of being." To the principle of air are ascribed the spirit, thinking and all mental and physical movements. Bile is associated with the will and the energetic and dynamic aspects of all physiological processes. Phlegm corresponds to feelings and to matter. Only if these principal energies are in balance can the seven basic tissues of the human organism function optimally. The seven basic tissues are lymph, blood, reproductive fluids, muscles, fatty tissues, bones and bone marrow.

The Causes of Illness

In addition to the three poisons of the mind, Tibetan medicine also recognizes secondary causes of illness, which include, among others:

- False expression of body, language and spirit, that is, excessive or suppressed expression.
- Wrong nutrition, that is, nutrition that does not correspond to one's own physical and nutritional type. Everyone is classified as one of seven types by Tibetan medicine.

- Climate and environment, to which everyone has to adjust his or her behavior. For example, settlement in polluted areas should be avoided, as should exposure of the body to harmful radiation.
- Astrological influences, which variously affect the causes of illness as well as the therapeutic measures chosen to counteract them.
- Bad karma. Since one of the pillars of Buddhist doctrine is reincarnation, karma plays a central role in Buddhist medicine. Tibetan doctors work on the assumption that some diseases are the result of karma, which is understood as the net result of accumulated actions, both positive and negative.

The Seven Physiological Types

Since each person has his or her own configuration of the three humors or principles of being, each person is different. To deal with this diversity Tibetan medicine has simplified and summed up the possible combinations into seven physical types.

The seven types are: 1. *Loong*, 2. *Tripa*, 3. *Begen*, 4. *Loong/Tripa*, 5. *Loong/Begen*, 6. *Tripa/Begen*, 7. *Loong/Tripa/Begen*.

Tibetan Diagnosis

Tibetan doctors diagnose without the use of tools, but they need to be highly trained, especially with respect to the sensitivity of their fingertips. There are four steps to a complete diagnosis, although pulse and urine analyses are the most important:

- Visual inspection of the tongue, urine, the veins

of the ear and the general physical appearance.
- Pulse diagnosis, which can accomplish two things: with healthy persons it is used to establish the physical type and thus to identify weaknesses in the system, which allows the used of preventive measures; with sick patients, pulse is used to diagnose pathology.
- Questioning the patient about her health history and that of her family.
- Physical examination, both specific and general.

The Holistic Basis of Tibetan Medicine

The goal of any Tibetan therapy is good health of the body and the spirit. The assumption is that any disturbance in the spiritual realm will have its impact on the physical body, and vice versa. In accordance with this holistic view, therapeutic methods are classified into three groups:

1. External Methods
   acupuncture, *Chug-Nye* massage, bloodletting, moxibustion, cupping, mineral baths, smoke therapy, *Kum-Nye* exercises, *Yantra* yoga, analytical meditation and cold waterfall therapy
2. Internal Methods
   herbal teas and pills, laxatives, emetics, expectorants, inhalation, enemas, fasts, diets and behavioral rules
3. Spiritual Methods
   religious practices, mantras, recitation of prayers, *Tum-mo* yoga meditation, spiritual meditation, visualization techniques, laying on of hands, chakra and color therapy, pilgrimages, prostrations and the circumambulation of sacred places

The Essential Herbs of Tibetan Medicine

Tibetans like to call their country the land of healing herbs. In fact, the huge Himalayan mountain range and the high plateau of Tibet are known for the variety and high quality of the medicinal herbs that grow there. In ancient Tibet some 2,200 healing plants and their variants were known, though only a part of each plant was used. Today about 150 plants remain in the Tibetan pharmacopoeia, producing about 200 remedies.

Tibetan Herbal Compounds

Unlike healing teas of the European tradition, which are usually made of a single plant, the medicinal recipes of Tibet are generally compounded of many different herbs. In fact, these Tibetan compound products can contain as many as a hundred ingredients, some of them powdered metal, stone and minerals. The idea behind this complexity is that the primary effect of the main ingredients needs to be "tamed, corrected and aligned." Thus the role of some substances in these recipes is just to reduce or cancel out the side effects of certain other ingredients.

The composition of these complex recipes is determined partly by their taste: sweet, tart, salty, bitter, sharp and astringent. Some plants heal "hot" illnesses while others heal the "cold" ones. What is also considered is the effect of each ingredient on specific humors. The following Tibetan medicinal plants are also classified by the criteria of the "Four Tantras." This work, probably written in the fourth century A.D., is the basic text of Tibetan medicine.

Costus Root

Saussurea costus This herb of the Asteraceae family has a stem two meters high. It grows in India, Pakistan, China and Tibet at altitudes between 2,500 and 4,000 meters, preferring the moist slopes of the northern Himalayas. Tibetan medicine calls this plant *ru-rta* and uses only the roots. The *Tantra of Explanations* classifies this herb among those that lower fever "in connection with wind."

Ru-rta alleviates bloating and the symptoms of diseases of the lungs and of diphtheria. It is also used with abscesses in the throat area and against "excessive growth of flesh." Modern science has confirmed the efficacy of the herb in these respects. The costus root contains an alkaloid called saussurine, which has been established as having a relaxing effect on the bronchial tubes and the gastrointestinal tract. Tibetan mothers massage the navels of their children with butter and *ru-rta*.

Bael Fruit

Aegle marmelos The original home of this deciduous tree was in the western Himalayas and in the forests of the Coromandel Ghats of India, but it is now also cultivated in eastern India and on the Sunda Islands. The tree grows at most to medium height and bears long, sharp thorns. The fruit is called *bil-ba* in Tibet. It is yellow-green or yellow-brown, globular or oval, and ranges in size from five to twelve centimeters. Tibetan medicine uses the ripe and the unripe fruit, the leaves, the roots and the blossom of the plant. Bael fruit is among those plants that can stop diarrhea. In Ayurveda too the unripe fruit is used to treat both chronic

diarrhea and dysentery. The ripe fruit, strangely enough, is effective against constipation.

Hedych Root

Hedychium spicatum Hedych is native to China and Indo-Malaysia, but it grows in subtropical and temperate regions of the Himalayas up to altitudes of 5,000 to 6,500 feet (1,500–2,000 m), in the Punjab and in Nepal. The plant grows up to 3 feet (1 m) high, but the parts used are subterranean, namely, the fleshy rhizomes. They are dried before being added to Tibetan remedies.

Camphor Tree

Cinnamomum camphora The evergreen camphor tree is a native of the Chinese hard-leaf forests. It can grow as tall as forty meters and develop enormous girth. Its gnarled branches bear long oval leaves. Oil of camphor is used in aromatherapy. The oil is obtained from the wood of the tree by steam distillation and subsequent sublimation, a process whereby the volatile oil is won directly from the solid wood and then collected in liquid form. Western herbal practitioners use camphor oil against colds and as a disinfectant. Tibetan medicine uses it for similar ends. As the most cooling substance in their pharmacopoeia, camphor is applied by Tibetan doctors to fight full-blown fevers, especially chronic, deep-seated ones. Camphor is also the basis for a mixture that cools and calms the gallbladder.

Chebalic Myrobalan or *Bedda* Nut Tree

Terminalia chebula This deciduous tree of medium height is called *a-ru-ra* in Tibet. It grows in many regions of Asia, in Malaysia no less than in north India, between Kangra and Bengal or in the highlands of Dacca. The *bedda* nut itself is a fruit, two to four centimeters long, usually oval, of yellow or black color. The fruit of the *myrobalan* tree is central to the Tibetan tradition because, beyond its other healing qualities, it is said to bestow long life. In depictions of the Buddha Shakyamuni, he is offering *bedda* nuts, symbols of the life that emanates from the Master of Healing. In the ancient Tibetan medical texts, eight varieties of the bedda nut are described: "victorious," "fearless," "nectar,"

"increasing," "dry," "small and black," "gold-colored" and "bird beak."

The "victorious" *bedda* nut was a miraculous, all-healing fruit that has now become extinct. In the taste of that fruit the gamut of all possible tastes was combined, except salty. Moreover, it had the power to heal diseases caused by wind, bile or phlegm, and those that are considered hot no less than those that are cold. Only the "gold-colored" *myrobalan* fruit comes close to this bounty of healing. All the other variants combine only five of the six tastes (salty is absent) and heal only illnesses of wind, bile and phlegm, and cannot work on both hot and cold conditions.

The "fearless" *myrobalan* fruit is black and elongated. It is used for ailments of the eye. The "nectar" *myrobalan* is yellow, with thick flesh. It helps the emaciated gain weight. The fruit called "increasing" has the shape of a vase; it is recommended for wounds. The flesh of the "dry" *bedda* nut is thin and wrinkled. It is able to heal gallbladder complaints in children. The "bird beak" variety is elongated and pointed and is used as a laxative. The one referred to as "small and black" has no seeds and its medicinal qualities resemble those of the "nectar" variety.

In addition to this important *myrobalan* tree, there are two other related plants, *Myrobalan belerica* and *Myrobalan emblica*. In the traditional texts the fruit of these three species are often encompassed by the phrase "the three fruits" (*bras-gsum*). In Ayurvedic medicine there is a corresponding concept, *triphala*. This trio of related fruit is recommended in both medical traditions as an effective internal purifier. Tibetan doctors also use the three fruits to make a medical butter recipe that will calm "disorders of wind."

Neem Tree

Azadirachta indica The neem tree, native to east India and Malaysia, is one of the most important trees of India. It is considered a holy tree and is often planted in gardens and village squares. It is a large, impressive evergreen, with sparse foliage. Its fruit is about 1 ½ centimeters long and contains one kernel. Something of a miracle tree, the neem offers all its parts for use, and the range of products made from it includes fertilizers, insecticides, dyes, waxes, lubricants, soaps and many other things.

For medical purposes the leaves, the flowers, the bark of roots and stems, and the fruit are all useful. In Indian medicine neem serves mostly to destroy internal parasites, to fight fevers and as a bitter. Westerners too have discovered the virtues of neem and use its extracts as an insecticide.

Tibetan medicine counts neem among the bitter herbs that are employed with gallbladder disease, eye diseases, all manner of fevers, loss of appetite and skin conditions, as well as in the fight against "demonic possession." Neem is supposed to be particularly effective against "fever of the bones." The tender leaves at the tips of branches calm the gallbladder and heal wounds.

Sandalwood

Pterocarpus Santalinus The original habitat of the sandalwood tree is in India, but because it is now a protected species, it is cultivated in many other places, including the Philippines. The tree reaches about seven meters in height. Its core wood or pith is red in color.

The medicines are made from the core wood, which is the layer of wood between the cambium and the heart of the tree. Tibetan medicine

classifies red sandalwood among the plants with an astringent effect, which will ease illnesses of a "hot nature" and diseases of the blood. Other medical traditions also esteem red sandalwood, especially as a remedy against ailments of the gastrointestinal tract, as a diuretic, blood purifier and reliever of coughs. The essential oil of white sandalwood is an important ingredient in perfumes with an oriental character.

Asafetida

Ferula asa-foetida Only the oily resin, won by tapping the rhizomes and roots of the plant, is used by the Tibetans. The resin is pressed into little cakes. Asafetida is used in "illnesses of cold," especially with "wind in the heart" and "disorders of the phlegm" with wind. As a healing substance asafetida is classed with medicines used to treat disturbances caused by micro-organisms. In this respect the Tibetan and Ayurvedic schools agree, as the latter uses the fetid resin to treat bloating and to improve the appetite, in other words, to treat problems of the digestion. Both traditions use asafetida with other gastrointestinal difficulties too, namely, serious constipation, colic and parasites.

MAGICAL TEAS FROM THE LAND OF SNOW-COVERED PEAKS

Drinking tea is a favorite occupation of Tibetans, and they indulge in it all day long. The basic ingredient of most Tibetan teas is green tea from China. The city of Tartsedo, on the former Tibet–China border, used to be the main marketplace for the precious commodity. It was here that the green tea leaves from China were crushed and ground small, fermented and then pressed into the famous Tibetan tea bricks. This process guaranteed that the quality of the tea remained stable till it reached the deepest recesses of the Himalayan state. The yak caravans of the Tibetan tea traders carried the tea over the high passes into the hinterland. More recently, tea has been successfully cultivated in the southern reaches of Tibet.

Bhö-cha, the Classic Tibetan Butter Tea

Mentioning tea and Tibet brings to mind the legendary butter tea, drunk in that country since time immemorial and offered to every guest as the traditional welcome. No book, no movie about the Himalayas has ever omitted *Bhö-cha*, which means simply "Tibetan tea." What makes this tea so famous—and infamous—is the addition of butter and salt. The resulting beverage is more like a savory soup than a tea. More and more Western travelers to the Himalayas return home wanting to taste this nourishing hot drink once more. *Bhö-cha* is the ideal shot in the arm for a people who live at an altitude of four thousand meters, in country so rugged that just going about your daily routine constitutes physical strain. And now it is high time that we dispelled one of the misunderstandings concerning this drink: it has been shunned by some because of false reports that it is made with rancid butter. The Tibetans use fresh butter.

> *5 g or 1 tbsp. tea, ground from the*
> *Tibetan tea brick*
> *2 oz. (50 g) butter*
> *6 oz. (⅕ l) whole milk*
> *1 hefty pinch of salt (a scant teaspoon)*
> *4 cups (1 l) cold water*
> (Variation: *Instead of butter and milk, it is*
> *possible to use heavy cream.*)

Preparation and use: Bring your piece of tea brick to a boil in the water, turn the heat down to low and simmer very gently for 10 to 15 minutes. The longer you simmer it, the more intense the tea will taste, but simmering will decrease its impact as a stimulant. If you need to wake up, remove the tea from the burner shortly after it has boiled. Strain the tea and add the butter, milk and salt. Now you are ready for the most important part: the Tibetans pour the tea into a special tea mixer, made of wood. They call this device a *dogmo* and the tea is pushed through it several times. The *dogmo* can be as long as a meter and is equipped with a plunger of corresponding length, which is used to push the tea mixture carefully up and down. This mixing job requires a certain dexterity and lots of practice, since the liquid is easily pushed out onto the floor. It is not easy to find a *Bhö-cha dogmo* in our latitudes, and so even natives of Tibet reach for the blender at this stage of the operation.

Cha-dhang
Meditation Tea

If butter tea does not turn out to be your cup of tea after all, try this variation on black tea. *Cha-dhang* is prepared without butter and is a stimulating drink. It is highly prized by the Buddhist monks, who use it to keep alert during the long hours they spend praying.

about 0.1 oz. (2 g) Tibetan tea brick
1 scanty tsp. salt
4 cups (1 l) cold water

Preparation and use: Follow the above instructions for butter tea, leaving out the butter, milk or cream.

Oh-cha Milk Tea

Oh-cha means "milk tea." This is the favorite tea of the Tibetan nomads, who keep yaks and therefore always have enough milk. This a very good drink for older people and children.

2 oz. (5 g) Tibetan tea brick
about 1 ⅓ cups (⅓ l) milk
1 scanty tsp. salt
4 cups (1 l) cold water

Preparation and use: As the foregoing two recipes, but using milk.

Dr. Shak's Tibetan Spice
and Herb Teas

The tea recipes that follow were put together by the Tibetan physician Kalsang Shak according to the principles of his medical tradition. Shak, who is trained as a naturopath, wants to share Tibetan philosophy and healing arts with the Western world. He maintains a center for Eastern healing methods in Baar, Switzerland. For his friends and patients he has developed a choice of four different herbal teas, prepared in strict accordance with Tibetan medical principles. Each tea contains up to thirty ingredients, whose effects are mutually aligned. Tibetan medical teas aim to harmonize the three bodily humors and thereby improve general well-being. Unfortunately, many of the components of these teas are completely unavailable in the West. To enjoy the original formulas you have to order them directly from Dr. Shak. (See the list of addresses at the back of the book.) For the readers of this book Dr. Shak has developed simplified versions of his recipes, and the ingredients for these teas can be obtained in any good herbalist's store or supply house.

Tashi-Delek
Daytime Tea

Tibetans say "*Tashi-Delek*" to one another a lot; it means "the blessings of luck and peace be with you." This tea fits any situation because it is aligned with the principles of the three bodily fluids as well as with the five elements of Tibetan medicine. Therefore, it harmonizes and regulates the whole organism. The tea is of great service particularly to those people whose nerves and emotional balance are under heavy stress from their hectic and overstimulating lifestyle. *Tashi-Delek* is refreshing and revitalizing. It is a pleasant beverage to sip at work.

For 1 cup (250 ml):
¼ tsp. powdered ginger
½ tsp. powdered licorice
1 tsp. dried stinging nettle
¼ tsp. dried lemon balm
1 cardamom pod, crushed in a mortar
1 dried apricot
1 cup (250 ml) water

Preparation and use: Combine all ingredients and pour boiling water over them. Cover and let steep for 5 to 10 minutes. Strain, pressing the ingredients a little with a spoon. If you want, you can sweeten this tea with honey or cane sugar.

Datsen Lady Tea

Datsen is the Tibetan word for the monthly cycle. Here we have a typical women's tea, suitable for females of all ages. Its aroma too is considered feminine; it is full and fruity. *Datsen* tea's special virtue is that it calms a system that is wrought up during menstruation.

For 1 cup (250 ml):
1 tsp. asparagus root powder
½ tsp. dried dandelion root
1 tsp. dried gooseberries
¼ tsp. turmeric powder
1 tiny pinch saffron
5 Szechuan peppercorns
1 cup (250 ml) water

Preparation and use: Combine all ingredi-

ents and cover with boiling water. Cover the container and steep 5 to 10 minutes. Strain the tea and press the dregs lightly with a spoon. You can sweeten this tea to taste with honey or cane sugar. Take 1 cup a day, as needed.

Metö Digestive Tea

Metö, the "heat of fire," refers to the fire of digestion, which plays a very central role in Tibetan healing. The smooth functioning of the entire digestive process is, in the thinking of Tibetan doctors, the key to health and well-being. *Metö* tea consists of a very spicy, prickly mix of spices and herbs that stimulate digestion.

For 1 cup (250 ml):
1 tsp. pomegranate seeds
1 tsp. chopped dried rosehips
¼ tsp. powdered ginger
1 cup (250 ml) water

Preparation and use: Combine all ingredients, pour the boiling water over them, cover the container, and steep 5 to 10 minutes. Strain the tea and press the dregs lightly with a spoon. You can sweeten this tea to taste with honey or cane sugar. After a rich meal enjoy a cup of *Metö* tea with dessert.

Gönka Wintertime Tea

Tibetans certainly know *gönka*—winter. At this time of year, when the days are cold and wet, we need a tea with warming qualities. The following recipe has all that and it strengthens the immune system, too, something that is sorely needed in the winter months.

For 1 cup (250 ml):
3 pieces tamarind
1 tsp. grated lemon rind
¼ tsp. ginger root, freshly grated or powdered
¼ tsp. fennel seeds
1 cup (250 ml) water

Preparation and use: Combine all ingredients, pour the boiling water over them, cover the container, and steep 5 to 10 minutes. Strain the tea and press the dregs lightly with a spoon. You can sweeten the tea to taste.

Sorig, the Tea from the Men-tsee-Khang

"*Sorig*" derives from "*gso-rig*," which means "the science of healing" and refers to Tibetan medicine. The recipe for this comforting tea derives from the famous Tibetan medical center in India, the Tibetan Medical and Astrological Institute in Dharamsala, also known as *Men-tsee-Khang*. Sorig is a holistic remedy against coughs, bronchitis, colds and flu. Tibetan doctors also recommend it to improve the appetite. The tea has no side effects at all and can be taken at any time of day. Children and adults, the sick and the well, can all enjoy this tea in liberal quantities.

1 tsp. Sorig *herb mixture*
1 cup (250 ml) water

Preparation and use: Measure the tea mixture into a pot or pan and pour boiling water over it. Cover and let steep for 5 minutes. Strain. Drink up to 3 cups a day.

Note to this recipe: *Men-tsee-Khang* was founded by the Dalai Lama in 1961 to preserve the Tibetan medical tradition after the Chinese occupied Tibet. In addition to the medical school and astrological studies, the institute maintains a research laboratory and a pharmacological factory, where Tibetan pills, "jewel pills," salves, incense sticks and teas are produced, and they can be ordered from there. (See list of suppliers at the back of the book.) The teas are sold under the brand name *Sorig*. The *Men-tsee-khang* also includes diagnostic and treatment clinics, a pharmacy and a hospital.

ARABIA

LIGHT FROM THE EAST
HEALING TRADITIONS OF ARABIA

Anyone intent on researching the healing "light from the East" is soon going to encounter Egyptian medicine. It is at the root of the medical arts practiced all over the Arab world.

Egyptian medicine—just like our own—derived largely from medical theories developed by the Greeks. The best-known physician of ancient Greece was Hippocrates (468–377 BC), whose code of medical ethics underlies the Hippocratic oath, still taken at some medical schools by students embarking on the study of medicine. A later Greek physician, Galen, who lived from AD 131 to 199, also influenced our traditions of healing. He practiced medicine in Rome.

On the work of these two ancient healers is based the theory of the four cardinal humors, which was set down in writing by Galen. According to this holistic view of health, four bodily fluids sustain our health: blood, mucus or phlegm, black bile and yellow bile. Each of these bodily fluids has its own set of qualities—cold, dry, hot or moist—and is ruled by one of the four elements, as follows:

- Blood is hot and moist; it is related to the element of air.
- Mucus is cold and moist; it is associated with the element of water.
- Black bile is cold and dry: it is ruled by earth.
- Yellow bile is hot and dry; it is under the rule of fire.

When a person's four humors are in balance, he or she is in good health. Galen went further, however, asserting that each human being tends to a certain kind of imbalance, and the habitual pre-dominance of this or that humor is what determines each person's basic temperament. An imbalance of the humors can also be caused by external factors, and the consequent overabundance or shortage of one of the humors is the cause of ill health. To cure disease, the original relative balance of the four humors has to be re-established. This theory of health classifies healing substances according to a similar set of qualities, and prescriptions are made up accordingly.

Very little has changed in the theoretical training of Arab doctors, the hakim, since Galen. *Hakim* means "sage or philosopher," and the word was applied to all health practitioners until the concept of a medical specialty arose. One of the main tenets of Arab medicine was that each illness has to be seen as a unique case, and all treatments are therefore custom-made. According to the writings of Hippocrates, the poor must be given medical treatment free of charge.

Since there were virtually no female doctors, women presented an abiding problem to Arab medicine: according to the tenets of Islam, a woman could not be examined by a man who was not a member of her own family. Should a doctor actually encounter a female patient, she remained hidden behind a veil or screen. Nor surprisingly, diagnosing invisible patients seldom met with success, and consequently, it was taken for granted that it was not worth dealing with female patients. When it came to delivering babies, midwives were responsible, and they received training from hakim.

All over the Arab world there were well-equipped hospitals, as, for example, in Baghdad, Damascus, Cairo and Marrakesh. Separate wards existed for men and for women. In Alexandria and southern Persia they even maintained med-

was done according to the teachings of another Greek scientist, Dioscurides, the author of *De Materia Medica*. His work, published in five volumes, was translated into Arabic, Syrian and Persian. Eventually, medicine was taught using the same texts wherever Islam was practiced, that is, in the vast territory from Andalusia to India.

There was already a lively trade in teas and healing herbs in ancient times. Writing in second-century Rome, Galen says about the provenance of the herbs that he uses, "… some of them are brought to me from greater Syria, others from Palestine, yet others from Egypt and from Cappadocia."

Earlier, in the days of the Pharaohs, the ancient Egyptians had used a multitude of herbs and spices for health and beauty. Medically speaking, the Egyptians had reached a very high level of development. In fact, historians conjecture that the population of Egypt was one of the most healthy in the entire ancient world. We do not know much about the indigenous medicine of ancient Egypt, but it is believed that it was a mixture of magic and tried-and-true domestic remedies. All Egyptian deities were responsible for the art of healing, and they were famous for their blessings far beyond the borders of Egypt. Some of our own knowledge of what Egyptian medicine was like comes from a text called the *Papyrus Ebers* and about a dozen others like it. It took much detailed work to decipher these manuscripts. We are indebted for much of our information to Galen, who was able to inspect many Egyptian sources that have since been lost or destroyed.

"Magic is effective with the medicine. The medicine is effective with the magic."

Papyrus Ebers

ical strongholds. Despite the great distances between them, these medical centers were in regular communication with one another, exchanging experiences and discoveries. With the expansion of Islam, Arab healing arts were transplanted to India, where they are still taught under the name of *Unani*. When *Unani* arrived in India, Ayurveda was already established there. The principles that underlie the two systems of medicine are similar (see pages 37 ff.), and in time there was some exchange of ideas.

Since dissecting the human body was strictly prohibited, surgery was practically impossible. As a consequence, Arab medicine fell back on strengthening the natural defenses of the body. Since the assumption was that the four bodily fluids were generated by the process of digestion, great emphasis was placed on a balanced diet and a healthy gastrointestinal tract. This is a view that seems to meet with increasing scientific support. In addition, many hakim considered the positions of the sun and moon when making their diagnoses.

Each remedy, be it derived from plants, animals or minerals, was chosen to harmonize with the temperament of the patient and to re-establish the disturbed equilibrium of the bodily fluids. This

THE CENTRAL HERBS AND SPICES OF ARAB MEDICINE

Generally, the influence of the Middle Eastern medical tradition on our own medical arts is underestimated. Since both systems arose from the same Greco-Roman roots, they have a lot in common. Many of the plants we now consider commonplace were originally used in the Levant. It is true that the infusions and decoctions so popular today with alternative medical practitioners and as home remedies were almost unknown in the old Arab world. Climate and geography could explain their absence: large expanses of desert, chronic water shortages, great heat, and the fact that many Arabs lived in nomadic tribes. Instead of teas, Arab healing drinks were based on wine, beer or mead, the healer mixing his herbs with these alcoholic beverages. Another way herbal remedies were administered was by cooking them along with other ingredients into a soup-like pap. An ancient Arab doctor might also have given you your medicine as candy: ground herbs were mixed with honey, formed into bite-sized balls and dried, so that they could be sucked.

One of the most important procedures of ancient Egyptian medicine was the clyster, or enema. Certain doctors specialized in mixing and administering enemas; they were the "shepherds of the behind." The Egyptians held that most of our complaints were caused by the food we ate, something to which much scientific research also attests. Suppositories and tampons were used in Egypt. It is a fact that many medical substances are best absorbed if taken anally. Salves and oils, compresses, poultices, gargles and sneeze powders were employed, as well as aromatherapy and smoke.

Wormwood

(*Also:* southern wood, mugwort and tarragon)
Artemisia The genus *Artemisia* includes a number of plants: wormwood, mugwort and tarragon are the best known. The botanical name of the family derives from the goddess Artemis. In Greece she was worshipped as the protector of virgins, in the Orient as the Queen of the Amazons. Mugwort and wormwood were regarded as the goddess's gift to women. Mugwort (*A. vulgaris*), probably one of the oldest healing plants in the world, was used to ease birthing and to regulate the monthly cycle. Wormwood (*A. absinthum*) was said to promote bleeding. Both plants, however, also lent themselves to the removal of unwanted pregnancies if one knew how to use them. While the use of mugwort was mostly restricted to obstetrics, wormwood had many other applications. The plant helped in getting rid of worms and against pain in the anal region. Moreover, wormwood was made into vermouth, a wine that served, among other things, as a remedy against fevers. The proverbially bitter taste of wormwood is also present in the wine.

In contrast to mugwort, southern wood (*Artemisia abrotanum*) was considered a male remedy. Its main benefit was its effect on sexual desire; it is called "old man." Tarragon (*Artemisia dracunculus*), a close relative of these herbs, remained in the kitchen.

Wormwood contains many bitter substances and a volatile oil, rich in thujon. If taken in large amounts this substance is intoxicating and hallucinatory. Constant use has devastating effects on the system. Absinthe, a potent liqueur formerly made from this plant, is now prohibited, but wormwood tea is acceptable, since the amount of thujon in an infusion is negligible.

It is best to leave mugwort alone. Pregnant women and those who wish to conceive should not even go near it.

Wormwood Tea for Stomach and Intestinal Discomfort
Pour hot water over half a teaspoon of dried wormwood, which can be found in some health food or herbal stores. Let the tea steep for 10 minutes, then strain and sip slowly. Sip a cup before meals, but do not overdo it, as too much wormwood will cause nausea, diarrhea and cramps.

Tarragon Tea Improves Your Appetite
Steep 1 teaspoon of tarragon from your spice shelf in boiling water for a few minutes. Drink before meals, and more frequently if desired.

Aniseed

Pimpinelle anisum Egyptian texts mention the use of aniseed and the healing powers of the herb. Among other things, anise is supposed to maintain youthfulness. The spice is won from the seed, and to this day it is an important part of Middle Eastern cuisine. Many people in the Orient chew a few anise seeds after meals, to promote better digestion.

Anise tea is helpful against bloating, stomach and intestinal problems, and stomach cramps. Steep 1 or 2 teaspoons of aniseed in a cup of boiling water for about 15 minutes. After straining, the tea can be sweetened with honey or sugar. You may consume 2 or 3 cups a day. Freshly ground anise is very good stirred with milk and honey. Anise tea was considered an aphrodisiac and was said to increase a man's sperm count. A very special anise tea can be found in health food stores, called Afeku tea; it contains anise, fennel and caraway.

Apple Tree

Malus sylvestris Historically, most of the apples eaten in Arab countries were grown in Palestine. Such imported apples were very precious, and the apple was a symbol for the sun. The fruit was certainly a food, but its medical properties were not completely clear to Arab healers. Apples do have many valuable chemical components, fruit acids, minerals, vitamins and pectin. There is truth in the saying that an apple a day will keep the doctor away. Health food stores sell apple teas, some of them organic.

Basil

Ocimum basilicum The herb originates in India, but it was brought to Egypt during the time of the Pharaohs. Its reputation as a healing herb was not very great, however; instead, it was used to keep away dragons and other unwanted demons. Today we know that the strongly aromatic oil of basil is antiseptic and strengthening to the gastrointestinal tract. It is also believed to stimulate libido, and milk production in breast-feeding mothers. It tastes particularly good fresh, on tomatoes or in a salad. A Persian delicacy is anise-basil, which can be ordered from one of the sources listed at the end of the book.

The colorful fruits and vegetables used in Middle Eastern cuisine:
cumin, star anise, saffron, turmeric, allspice, pepper, cloves, cinnamon, tamarind and carob. In the background, pomegranate and jasmine.

Basil Tea for Overeating and Bloating
You can buy basil tea in bags. Or, you can pour boiling water over 2 teaspoons of dried basil, cover and steep for 15 minutes. Strain the tea. Drink 2 or 3 cups a day, always freshly brewed.

Basil–Almond Milk
Blend a handful of fresh basil leaves, 1 tablespoon of honey, 1 tablespoon of almond paste and ½ cup (125 ml) milk until there is almost no trace of the leaves. Add 2 cups (½ l) more milk and blend again.

Henbane

Hyoscyamus In ancient Greece and Rome, henbane was considered an important medical plant. It was also renowned as a magic herb. It has a strongly narcotic effect. The essential oil of *Hyoscyamus* is rubbed on rheumatic limbs and used for erotic massage. (For more on this herb, see page 128.)

Fenugreek

Trigonella foenum-graecum See page 140.

Dill

Anethum graveolens Dill is also an ancient spice. Dill is mentioned in four-thousand-year-old Arabic texts on healing plants. It is said that dill protects against spells and black magic. Above all, however, it alleviates and heals intestinal problems. If you want to treat your gastrointestinal problems with dill, try this dill water: 1 tablespoon dill seeds (fresh from your garden if available) are crushed in a mortar and then briefly boiled in 4 cups (1 l) water. Let this steep for 3 hours, strain and sweeten to taste with honey. Take 1 teaspoon, 3 times a day.

Oak

Quercus The oak tree has been an object of worship in many cultures, not least because huge, thousand-year-old oaks used to be a common, awe-inspiring sight. The oak has always been regarded as a life-giving, auspicious tree. It was said to bestow fertility. Acorns and oak bark were used in remedies against inflammations of the lower abdomen. And of course oak bark was used for tanning hides, as far back as ancient Egypt.

Oak Bark for Inflammation
You can find prepared oak bark in some herbal stores. Simmer 2 teaspoons of oak bark for 3 to 5 minutes in 1 cup (250 ml) water. This decoction can be drunk as a tea.

To make a gargle, which can be used against gingivitis but not swallowed, use 2 tablespoons of oak bark with 2 cups (500 ml) water and simmer for 15 to 20 minutes.

Vervain

Verbena officialis Vervain played an important role in the worship of the Egyptian goddess Isis. In ancient Rome they made love potions of vervain and myrtle. Vervain's medicinal properties were highly valued as well. It was used with inflammations, to heal wounds and to lower fever. Ready-to-make vervain tea is available in health food stores; it is also possible to buy the dried herb, *Verbena herba*, loose in herbal stores.

Fennel

Foeniculum vulgare Fennel was used by Egyptian doctors of the late Pharaonic period to cure diseases of the eye. The seeds were used to stimulate digestion. The old Egyptian custom of using fennel, a symbol of fertility, to obtain chil-

dren magically has been preserved among the witches of northern Italy.

Grains

Hordeum vulgare = Barley; *Triticum monococcum* = Emmer; *Triticum durum* = Hard Wheat; *Avena sativa* = Oats In ancient Egypt the cultivation of emmer and barley formed the basis of the economy. They were used to make bread and beer. Beer was one of the most important solvents for the components of healing herbs. Beer made of wheat contains yeast and is particularly well suited to medicinal purposes. In certain situations grains were used as a medium of exchange. Oat straw tea can be obtained in prepared form in health food stores.

Cloves

Syzygium aromaticum Like many other spices, cloves are of Chinese origin, but thousands of years ago their cultivation was already widespread all over Asia Minor. The clove is the closed flower bud of an evergreen tree. It has a positive, calming effect upon the psyche; it also alleviates pain. An effective analgesic can be made by crushing three or four cloves in a mortar, pouring a cup of boiling water over them, and placing a plate on the cup for twenty minutes while the tea is steeping. Drink a small glass of the strained tea twice daily on an empty stomach.

Pomegranate

Punica granatum The pomegranate tree is native to the Far East, but since ancient times it has been grown on the island of Cyprus. The flower and the fruit symbolize the two sexes, male and female. Many scholars believe that the pomegranate was the tree of knowledge and that Eve offered Adam a pomegranate, not an apple. Greek legend has it that the pomegranate originated from the blood of the god Dionysus. Wine made of the seeds was considered an aphrodisiac. The blossoms and the bark of the tree were used by Egyptian doctors to treat gastrointestinal problems and worms. The pressed juice is effective against inflammations of the gums, fevers and colds.

The use of pomegranate blossoms and fruit in healing was taken over by the Jews of that period. To this day in Palestine they make a refreshing summer drink out of these ingredients. The cordial syrup, grenadine, consisting of pomegranate and sugar, used to be considered a serious fever remedy, but today it is used mostly in cocktails.

Pomegranate Blossom Tea

Pour a cup of boiling water over 1 teaspoon of dried pomegranate blossoms, strain immediately and allow to cool before drinking. This tea was used against diarrhea and dysentery. Obtaining pomegranate blossoms may be difficult, but it is possible to grow a tree in a container, and if you look after it well, it will bloom.

Camomile

In ancient Egypt camomile was called the gift of the gods. It was worshiped as being the flower of the sun god, Ra. Camomile also had its place in the heavens of the old Germanic gods, where it was the flower of spring, the flower sacred to the god of light, Baldur.

Arab physicians of ancient times administered oil of camomile against pain. The plant was also used in cases of jaundice and kidney disease, and to assuage swelling of the gums. A salve of camomile for the cosmetic treatment of the complexion also goes back as far as Egyptian times. The skin of mummies was rubbed with a camomile cream. Greek and Roman medicine recommended camomile tea against inflammations. The fragrant plant was also used to calm fidgety and irritable people, to induce sleep and to ease the discomforts of menstruation.

To this day camomile is considered one of the most effective healing herbs. It is our favorite home remedy against all aches and pains. Camomile has been shown to calm jittery nerves and to help insomniacs. There is no substitute for camomile in Mother's treatment of wounds and colds. Science has recently been proving the ancient healers right.

Dried camomile blossoms and Roman

Oriental Chicken Breast with Camomile

This is a fast and healthful dish for special occasions.

4 chicken breasts
3 tbsp. camomile blossoms
3 cups (750 ml) chicken broth
1 stick cinnamon
½ cup (100 ml) white wine
½ tsp vermouth
4 egg yolks
4 zucchini
1 oz. (30 g) butter
2 tbsp. pink peppercorns
salt and pepper

Heat the chicken broth and simmer the camomile and pink peppercorns for 2 minutes. Add the chicken breasts and simmer till they are done, about 10 minutes. While the chicken is cooking, julienne the zucchini and set aside. When done, remove the chicken from the broth and keep warm. Place about ½ cup (125 ml) of the cooking liquid in a saucepan with the cinnamon stick and reduce by about half. Add the wine and vermouth, and boil vigorously to reduce it again. Remove the cinnamon. Braise the zucchini in the butter and season. Keep warm. Finish the sauce by putting the egg yolks into the top of a double boiler with the remaining chicken broth and adding the hot sauce in a thin stream, while beating vigorously over hot water till the sauce thickens. Season and serve the sauce over the chicken breasts, each on a bed of zucchini.

camomile are available everywhere. No family pantry should be without its box of camomile tea.

To prepare a brew of chamomile, proceed as follows: steep 1 tablespoon of camomile flowers in hot water for 10 minutes, then strain.

To prepare an inhalant for respiratory congestion, steep 2 tablespoons of camomile in a bowl with some boiling water and let it sit, covered, for a few minutes. When the heat is bearable to the patient, let him breathe in the steam under a towel.

Camomile/Caraway Tea

This tea will lessen pain and help during menstruation. Prepare the camomile tea as usual, but add some crushed caraway seeds. Drink it hot, in small sips. One or two cups a day should be enough, as camomile should not be taken in excess or for long periods. Overuse could lead to inflamed mucus membranes and cause jitteriness.

Cardamom

Elettaria candamomum The reed-like perennial cardamom is a native of India, but its seed was beloved by the Arabs, even way back in ancient times. To this day they spice their coffee with cardamom (see page 75). Medicinally, cardamom was used to stimulate circulation, hormonal activity and the whole metabolism. To sweeten the breath, people used to chew cardamom pods. You can improve your appetite by drinking the following tea: brew 1 teaspoon of ground cardamom seeds and 1 teaspoon of dried peppermint leaves for about 5 minutes, add a little honey and drink in small sips before meals. Drinking a pinch of ground cardamom in milk and honey will give the hormonal system a boost.

Chaste Tree

Vitex agnus-castus This plant was known to the ancient Egyptians. It was prescribed against madness, especially lunatic raving. On the one hand the plant was used to help monks to remain celibate, while on the other hand aphrodisiac potions were made of it. In this respect the plant was said to be very effective, especially in the Moroccan version of the recipe. The seed does contain a chemical substance that resembles steroids and can act as a natural stabilizer of the hormonal system. Vitex has become one of the most successful medications in the alternative gynecological pharmacopoeia. Capsules of chaste tree are available without prescription in health food stores.

Coriander

Coriandrum sativum Coriander grew in all parts of Egypt and the Near East in ancient times. The first mention of coriander occurs about 1500 BC, in an Egyptian papyrus; subsequently, it figures in Egyptian scrolls as an ingredient in numerous medical recipes. Coriander seeds were found in Tutankhamen's tomb. The herb was used primarily as an antacid. In Morocco, coriander is still used to exorcise demons that possess the patient and cause nervous agitation. Science has taught us that coriander loosens cramps, is mildly stimulating and is antibacterial.

Coriander Drinks

To heighten the lust for life: Crush 2 to 3 teaspoons of coriander seeds and soak them in 4 cups (1 l) wine in the refrigerator for 1 week. Strain and store this liquid. Drink small glasses at room temperature.

Against migraine: Crush 2 teaspoons of coriander seeds and steep in a cup of boiling water. After 10 or 15 minutes strain the tea. You can take several freshly prepared cups of this tea per day.

The Arabs like to spice many of their tasty teas with star anise.

Cumin

Cuminum cyminum At the time the pyramids were built, the Egyptians were already using cumin to heal. It is useful against a variety of complaints, especially diseases of the lungs. Cumin is cultivated in Egypt, Morocco and Syria.

Cumin Drink
Briefly heat 1 teaspoon of cumin seeds in a dry pan, then crush and steep in hot water for a short time. Season the tea with a touch of lemon juice and salt.

Linden

Tilia Although even the Greeks considered linden blossoms to be an old remedy, there is very little in the ancient medical literature about which ailments they cured with it. The Egyptians made mention of it, so it is probable that dried linden blossoms were imported to their empire.

In the West too, linden blossom tea is regarded as an old friend. We use it against coughs, colds, fever and sleeplessness.

Marjoram and Oregano

Marjorana hortensis, Origanum Marjoram and oregano belong to the same family of plants and they resemble each other. Marjoram is of Egyptian origin. Its strong fragrance alone is said to protect against diseases. Both herbs lower cholesterol levels and help in the reduction of fatty tissues. They also stimulate the digestion. Their antibacterial powers are considerable.

Arabian marjoram is one of the most popular culinary herbs of the Middle East. It grows wild in the hot and dry desert regions of that part of the world, and the more arid the climate, the stronger marjoram's taste. Desert people, who call it *zatar*, use it freely throughout all Arab countries and Israel. It is thought that Arabian marjoram is the plant the Bible mentions as "hyssop" (see page 77). There is also a Syrian marjoram. (See the list of suppliers at the end of the book.) Marjoram gives respite from cold symptoms.

Ephedra or Sand Cherry

Ephedra According to ethnopharmacologists, ephedra, also called sand cherry or sea grape, is among the very oldest of mankind's many ritual plants. Not much has come down to us about its medicinal uses. Mainly it was made into wine, which seems to have been very strong: it could

drive a person into a state of raving madness. In Cyprus they gave birthing mothers sand cherry tea to speed up the delivery. Today we know that all species of ephedra constrict the blood vessels, raise blood pressure and accelerate the circulation. They also stimulate the nervous system and loosen cramps, especially those of the respiratory passages. The active ingredient, ephedrine, is found in many cough medicines. Extract of sand cherry is considered an aphrodisiac, especially for women.

You can buy the herb in some herbal stores. For sand cherry tea, steep 1 heaping teaspoon of the dried herb in ¼ l water for 10 minutes. It soothes all ailments of the respiratory system. You can add cardamom, anise and fennel seeds to the tea, for their effect and flavor.

Mint

Mentha The many different varieties of mint are counted among the most ancient remedies used by mankind. From earliest times they were employed to soothe the stomach and for various gastrointestinal complaints. In this respect nothing has changed. With mint oil and mint tea ancient physicians also treated backaches, cough and bronchitis. This is how mint oil used to be obtained: Fresh mint leaves were pressed to release their juice; about half a cup might be sufficient. The juice was mixed with olive oil and the container placed in the sun for two weeks.

For mint tea, 1 tablespoon of mint leaves are steeped in a cup of boiling water for 5 to 10 minutes, and the tea is strained. You can drink 3 to 4 cups a day. In the Middle East, mint leaves are often added to green or black tea (see page 80).

Nutmeg

Myristica fragans Nutmeg is the seed of the nutmeg apple, the fruit of *Myristica fragrans*, the nutmeg tree. A native of the Indonesian Molucca Islands, the nutmeg was traded all over the ancient world and found a congenial home in the Levant, where it is widely cultivated to this day. Overdo nutmeg and you will experience a disagreeable high; it can even kill you.

Used in moderation, nutmeg has an impressive array of medical applications, as with chronic lung conditions, rheumatism and gout. It is said to eliminate toxins from the body very efficiently and to have a beneficial impact on the liver.

Nutmeg tea is very simple to make: to a cup of your favorite tea add a bit of honey and a small pinch of nutmeg. Drink only 1 cup per day. If you want to clear out your liver, drink this tea daily for 2 weeks, but not for longer.

Orchid

Orchis, Serapias The name "orchid" derives from the Greek word for testicle, *orchis*. It was called "boy's herb"—in Arabic, *salep*—because of the extraordinary aphrodisiac powers ascribed to it. In Greece there are people who make a living selling *salepi*, a drink reminiscent of coffee that they prepare from the roots of orchids. Occasionally, you may find salep powder in a Turkish store. In the past, orchid has also been used in a tonic that soothes gastrointestinal complaints.

Salep Drink
Mix 1 teaspoon of salep powder with 1 cup of cold milk. Bring to a boil and serve sprinkled with cinnamon.

Peony

Paeonia officinalis We are talking here about the peony that grows in your garden. Its name goes back to that of Paieon, physician to the Greek gods. Peony is also said to have a mystical connection to the moon. In the European tradition, peony was believed to be effective against illnesses caused by witches (see page 17). In fact, peony can relieve pain and loosen cramps. Peony blossom tea is sold in health food stores. However, it is not clear how best to use it.

Rue

Ruta graveolens Consult pages 134 ff.

Calming Rue Tea
This tea is brewed from a herbal mixture of equal parts dried rue, valerian, balm, hawthorn, dried mistletoe twigs, and caraway seeds. You may wish to have your herbalist prepare it for you and to use his or her directions to make the tea. This is not a tea to drink on a regular basis.

Rose

Rosa In ancient Egypt, rose was regarded as a universal healing herb. Roses were "the fragrance of the gods," and they had to be imported, so great was the demand for them. Rose oil, rosewater and rose tea were all extremely popular. The rosehip was used as an energizer, and no wonder: rosehips are very high in vitamin C and other vitamins, minerals, fruit acids and tannins.

Karkade—the Ruby Red Tea Made of Rosehips
You may be able to find this special oriental tea in your health food store, or you may wish to order it directly from Salus (see list of suppliers in the back of the book). Karkade tea contains the most fragrant spices of the Orient, plus rosehip, hibiscus flowers, blackcurrants and apple. Follow the instructions on the package to make this delicious tea.

Rosemary

Rosmarinus officinalis Several legends explain the origin of rosemary. One says that a deserving Assyrian youth, pursued by his enemies, prayed to the gods, who turned him into a rosemary bush. Rosemary was a favorite plant with the ancient Egyptians. Its active ingredients stimulate, strengthen the heart, loosen cramps and kill germs.

You can find rosemary tea ready to buy in health food stores. It is particularly useful when you suffer from some disturbance of the gastrointestinal tract. You can also use the herb off your spice shelf: Steep 1 teaspoon of rosemary needles in 1 cup of boiling water for about 15 minutes (covered). Strain your tea and drink it warm. You can make up to 3 fresh cups a day.

In Greece they drink a rosemary wine, which is supposed to support a weak heart. It is made by placing a few twigs of fresh rosemary in a bottle of white wine and letting it soak for a few days. A small glass a day does indeed assist the heart.

Saffron

Crocus sativus Saffron is the most expensive spice in the world. Its name comes from the Arabic word "*safaran*," which refers to yellowness. Saffron consists of the stigmata of the saffron crocus, which have to be harvested patiently by hand. Its fragrance is intense, its

color orange-red. A papyrus from Thebes outlines the healing powers of saffron. Its virtues are listed as follows: it strengthens the heart, filling it with warmth, augments sensuality, boosts sexual desire and increases male potency. It is also said to remove irregularities of the menstrual cycle.

Saffron Drink

Take a pinch each (about ¼ teaspoon) of the following spices: cinnamon, cardamom, ginger powder, pepper, cloves, nutmeg and saffron. It is best to use whole crushed cloves, cardamom and pepper, and to grind the nutmeg fresh. Add all this to your black tea and steep for 3 minutes, as usual. Strain and sweeten with honey. This tea should arouse the passions of persons of either gender.

Saffron Milk

Bring 1 cup (250 ml) milk to a boil. Add a pinch of saffron and keep the milk hot for another 2 or 3 minutes, until the saffron dissolves. Sweeten with honey. One cup a day should be sufficient.

Nigella

Nigella sativa This plant was recently rediscovered by Western scholars. Its place was firmly established in Egyptian medicine. The prophet Muhammad (570–632) is quoted in the Muslim book *Hadith* as saying: "*Nigella sativa* heals any illness—except death."

Nigella was also used as a cosmetic. It is said that Nefertiti's queenly complexion was due to her use of nigella oil. Cleopatra too is reported to have known about this beauty secret. In Tutankhamen's tomb a container of nigella oil was discovered; in his lifetime his personal physicians would offer him nigella seeds to chew after a heavy meal, to aid his digestion.

Nigella continued to be regarded as a heal-all by doctors in Greece and Rome, and throughout the Middle Ages. Today it is recommended against neuro-dermatitis and allergies, for it has recently been discovered that the chemical agents in nigella can normalize some of the extreme reactions of the immune system that characterize allergies. People who suffer from nervous skin diseases and allergies that affect the skin may benefit from nigella therapy.

Nigella Tea: The Secret of the Pharaohs

For 1 glass of tea, use 1 tablespoon of nigella seeds. Steep for 10 minutes before serving. The fragrance that rises from the tea brings to mind desert caravans and nomadic tents.

Licorice Root

Glycyrrhiza glabra For thousands of years man has employed licorice as a medical herb and as a spice. Not much is known about its healing properties, though it is a fact that it

Coffee with the Fragrance of the Orient

Coffee lovers can try adding a small pinch (¼ teaspoon) of ground nigella to their cup before serving. It is also possible to flavor your coffee by adding nigella to the grinder and letting it spin with the coffee beans. In the Levant it is an old custom to spice coffee with a pinch of ground cardamom; this is a particularly apt combination of flavors. Cardamom increases the flow of saliva and supports the digestion.

relieves thirst. Licorice helps with colds and bronchial inflammations.

Licorice Tea

Peel and crush 1 oz. (30 g) licorice root. Bring to a boil in 2 cups (500 ml) water and simmer for 5 minutes. Strain and drink a small glass before meals when you have a cold. When you feel very tense and stressed-out, dissolving a stick of licorice in hot water and sweetening it with honey makes a drink you can sip slowly to calm your nerves.

Tamarisk

Tamarix The feathery tamarisk grows along the Nile; it is mentioned in ancient Egyptian texts. In Morocco they still treat stomach complaints and intestinal problems with tamarisk. In the field of cosmetics, it is added to hair care products. You can drink tamarisk tea to relieve inflammations.

Thyme

Thymus In ancient Egypt the embalming salve rubbed on mummies contained thyme. The herb, which has very powerful anti-inflammatory and antibacterial virtues, was also applied to skin lichen. Tea of thyme can be bought in the health food store, but you can use the herb off your kitchen shelf. Just steep 1 teaspoon of thyme for 10 minutes and strain. Drinking several cups a day will help with sore throats and coughs.

Frankincense

Olibanum Frankincense was used not only to make an offering of smoke but also as a healing agent. An old recipe states that 2 cups (500 ml) of wine was brought to a boil with 1 tablespoon of olive oil, 1 tablespoon of honey and 2 or 3 kernels of frankincense. The drink was then bottled. Half a shot glass in the morning and in the evening was supposed to strengthen the heart.

Hyssop

Hyssopus Hyssop is a herb of the *labiatae* family of plants. It is esteemed by herbal healers for its many medicinal qualities. Tea of hyssop is a mild cardiac tonic and helps with breathlessness.

Hyssop is mentioned in the Bible. "Take hyssop and sprinkle me, that I may be clean; wash me, that I may become whiter than snow" (Psalm 51:7). Scholars question, however, whether the plant in question is really *Hyssopus* or another species of the same botanical family, namely, marjoram—a suggestion made in the New English Bible. Whatever may be the reasoning of biblical scholars, there certainly is a variety of marjoram that thrives in the arid deserts of that region. It is called *zatar* in Arab countries and in Israel.

The German author Kurt Allgeier has written a book about biblical medicine. He believes that all the healing herbs mentioned in the Bible were brought by the Israelites from Egypt. He suggests that they learned about the Egyptian healing arts during their years in captivity. Mr. Allgeier also makes the important point that the Bible interprets medical knowledge in its own way, not at all the way we think of medicine today. "The Bible turns healing plants and medicinal recipes into something very different. In the Bible we encounter an understanding of nature that is far above what we mean by nature and

natural healing power." Underlying the cure—underlying health—is wholeness. What the Bible understood as true healing was the power of God entering the patient. Healing plants were not just remedies or mere sources of chemical components that effect a cure; plants were revered as carrying concentrated life force, as bearers of divine grace.

On the subject of hyssop and marjoram there is another editorial footnote in the New English Bible, in the following passage from John 19:29: "A jar stood there, full of sour wine; so they soaked a sponge with the wine, fixed it on a javelin and held it up to his lips." Here the footnote says that the word "javelin" might be "marjoram." Now, among the curative powers of marjoram and hyssop was said to be their stupefying effect when the herb was boiled in acid. It was given to the mortally wounded and the crucified to ease their suffering. So it has been argued by some that the soldiers did not wish to mock Christ; on the contrary, they wanted to help him bear his pain.

Another plant mentioned in the Bible as having beneficial effects is the *daroo* tree, the Egyptian or Oriental sycamore (*Ficus sycamorus*). A tea was made from this plant by briefly boiling in water its dried or fresh leaves. It was said to clean stomach and intestines. A tea made of the bark was a common laxative. It was brought to a boil in water and allowed to steep for a while.

Cinnamon

Cinnamomum zeylanicum Cinnamon was among the first spices used by man. It is mentioned in the Bible. In addition to the Ceylon cinnamon tree, there is another variety of the plant, *Cinamomum cassia*, the bark of which is often sold as the spice, but it is not as fragrant and its healing properties are unknown. Oriental doctors utilized the Ceylon variety both in salves and for more occult purposes. Cinnamon stimulates the circulation and is antiseptic. Eating some cinnamon was thought to speed up recovery after an illness; the spice was mixed with drinking water to kill germs.

In Europe, where cinnamon was imported at great expense from the Levant and India, doctors used to regard it as a "purifier" for the whole body. It was also believed to build up potency and to energize the flow of bile. This is probably why it is a traditional ingredient in Christmas baking throughout Europe: it would help in the digestion of all that rich holiday fare.

Biblical Cinnamon Drink

As a tonic for the stomach and circulation you can try this recipe, based on ancient Oriental models. Bring 2 cups (500 ml) water to a boil with 3 cinnamon sticks and allow it to simmer for 10 minutes. Remove the cinnamon and add 2 cups (500 ml) red wine. Drink half a shot glass in the morning and evening.

PARADISAL TEAS FROM 1001 NIGHTS

Oriental Black Tea Mixtures

Traditionally, the favorite drink of Arabs was an infusion of sharp mint or, in the winter, of wormwood. It was to soften the harsh bitterness of both these beverages that tea was brewed and used to dilute them. One pot would contain green or black tea, the other mint or wormwood tea, and each guest would mix his drink according to taste, in his own glass.

Tea arrived in Asia Minor and the north of Africa over the ancient trade routes quite early in history. The plant is first mentioned outside the countries of its origin by an Arab trader, a certain Suleiman. In his report about China and India, he wrote in AD 851: "It is a plant with more leaves than clover and a more powerful fragrance too, but it tastes very bitter. Water is boiled and poured over it." He reports that in China, "… among the King's most important sources of revenue are salt and a herb, which they drink with hot water, which is very expensive, but its use is nonetheless widespread."

Although tea is now considered a classic drink of the Near East, at first it was dismissed as an exotic curiosity. It was quite insignificant in comparison with the trade in spices, silk and precious stones. The Levantine traders were acknowledged as important intermediaries between East and West; after all, they carried not only goods but also strange information and even philosophies. The famous Silk Road went through Isfahan, but for a long time the Muslim world displayed no interest at all in black tea. They drank—and still drink—mint tea. Today, however, black tea constitutes the greater part of their tea mixtures.

International tea statistics show just how important tea has become to the Arab world. Kuwait is first among tea-drinking nations, with an average annual per capita consumption of 1 ½ pounds (5.23 kg). Surprisingly, the British and Irish are only in second place, averaging about 6 ½ pounds (3 kg) per person per year. Syrians are next with just under 4 ½ pounds (2 kg), followed by Iranians and Tunisians with about 3 ½ pounds (1.5 kg).

Moroccans also drink tea at every possible occasion and at all times of day. It has to be hot and sweet. What Moroccans particularly appreciate is green tea with sugar, spiced with fresh mint leaves, which they call *nanah* in Arabic. Guests are offered this tea on the finely engraved metal trays that are used everywhere. The rules of hospitality require to this day that a guest be served three cups of tea on arrival, the last being the strongest. This ceremony allows the visitor to rest before doing anything else. In the era of the caravans it was customary to allow the guest to rest for three days after his grueling travels, before any dialogue could begin.

Components and Effect of Black Tea

Worldwide, black tea is the most-used beverage after water. It has entered the everyday routine of so many countries around the globe that we have forgotten that, originally, tea was used as a medicinal plant.

Black tea is the leaf of the shrub *Camilla sinensis*. Native to the mountains of Southeast Asia, the tea shrub has been cultivated in various parts of east Asia for over two thousand years, for both its leaves and its tender shoots. Legend has it that the Emperor Shen-nung

discovered tea in the year 2737 BC. It is said that he was drinking hot water when some leaves of the shrub happened to fall into his cup. He drank it and was enchanted by the improvement wrought to his drink by this mysterious leaf. At first, the Chinese used tea in healing. It was employed against tumors, abscesses, bladder ailments and lethargy. Only later did they become fond of tea as a refreshing beverage.

The two most important chemical components of tea are caffeine and tannins. Various volatile oils account for the aroma and taste. About four hundred aromatic substances have been identified as adding to the overall fragrance of the various teas grown worldwide. Other active ingredients in tea include fluoride, potassium, manganese, theophylline, theobromine and some B-complex vitamins.

There is very little chemical difference between the caffeine contained in tea and that in coffee, but in contrast to the caffeine carried by coffee, that found in tea does not have an adverse effect on the heart and circulation. Instead, the caffeine in tea promotes blood flow to the brain and aids its functions. It acts directly on centers of thought and feeling and on the central nervous system. Tea is therefore a good stimulant for those who do mental work. Scientific research has shown that tea speeds the processes of learning and improves memory. To the tannin in tea, scientists ascribe a healing capacity against ailments of the intestinal tract. The minerals enable beneficial enzymes to be activated, help with lowering cholesterol levels and—believe it or not—reduce cavities. Theophylline expands the arteries, acts as a diuretic and strengthens the heart muscle, while B-vitamins heighten vitality.

How Long Should Tea Be Allowed to Steep?

Three minutes: The effect is stimulating. The caffeine is completely dissolved, but not all the tannins are present in the infusion.
Five minutes: The tea has a calming effect without having lost its ability to stimulate. The helpful tannins are all dissolved.

Moroccan Tea

Green tea—preferably gunpowder tea—is placed in a pot and, with a small amount of water, very briefly brewed. This first infusion is immediately discarded and the pot is filled with boiling water. This time the tea is steeped for a few minutes. The tea is served in glasses over mint leaves. The mint should be fresh, if possible. The tea is well sweetened. Black tea can be substituted for the green with equal success.

Iranian Tea

You will need 4 cups (1 l) milk and 2 level tablespoons of black tea. Bring the milk to a boil and pour over the tea leaves in the pot. Allow to steep for 5 minutes and serve. Sweeten to taste.

Cinnamon Tea

Make your black tea as usual. Add a sprinkle of cinnamon and some honey to each cup. Each guest uses a cinnamon stick to stir the tea and can add more honey as desired.

Nomad Tea

Brew 6 teaspoons of black tea with 4 cups (1 l) boiling water as you usually would. Place a slice of orange in each tea glass, pour the hot tea over it and offer sugar or honey as a sweetener. Serves 6.

Desert Tea

Steep 12 teaspoons of tea with boiling water for 5 minutes. Cut candied ginger into small pieces and add a few to each cup. Fill the cups only halfway with the hot tea. Pass around another pot with hot water so that each guest can determine the strength of his own brew. Yields 9 to 12 cups.

Oriental Tea

Brew 6 teaspoons of tea with 3 cups (750 ml) boiling water. After the tea has steeped, add the juice of 1 orange and ½ lemon and some ground lemon peel to the strained tea in the pot. Cut a fresh orange into 6 slices and stick 2 whole cloves in each slice. Place an orange slice in each cup and pour the hot tea over it. Sweeten to taste. Makes 6 small cups.

Spice Tea with Cream

3 cups (750 ml) water
10 tsp. of your favorite black tea
3 ½ oz. (100 g) brown rock candy
1 cup (250 ml) pineapple juice
juice of 2 oranges
1–2 sticks cinnamon
3 whole cloves
3 coriander seeds
3 allspice berries

1 large tart apple
1 cup (250 ml) whipped cream

Steep the tea for 3 minutes and strain into a pot. Add all but a small piece of the rock candy, the orange and pineapple juices, 1 or 2 broken cinnamon sticks and the spices. Peel the apple and grate it into the tea. Reheat the tea, but do not boil. Let it sit for 15 minutes. Crush the remaining rock candy very fine. Strain the tea and pour it into heat-resistant glasses. Arrange a white cap of whipped cream on top of each cup and sprinkle with the crushed rock candy. Serves 4 to 6.

Icy Specialties

Spiced Ice Tea

Steep 6 teaspoons of your usual tea in 3 cups (750 ml) water. Continue steeping for 5 more minutes with the addition of ¼ teaspoon each of allspice and cinnamon and a speck of nutmeg. Filter this tea and, while still warm, add ¾ cup (175 ml) fine sugar and 1 cup (250 ml) each of orange and lemon juice. Pour over 1 ½ cups (375 ml) crushed ice and serve. Yields 6 servings.

Mint Tea over Ice

Pour 3 cups (750 ml) boiling water over 6 teaspoons green tea leaves and allow to steep. Cool the strained tea and pour over ice cubes. To each glass add a cube of sugar and a mint leaf. Serves 6.

Oriental Love Potions

An important branch of ancient medicine was the art of mixing love potions, concoctions that would have an aphrodisiac effect on a lover. It is now assumed by scholars that a body of literature on this subject existed in Egypt. Oriental incense, with its sexually intoxicating emanations, found its way into the Greek world as well. Moreover, consciousness-expanding drugs had a solid place in the realm of religion/medicine. From India came the drug soma; Persia supplied its close relative, *Haoma* (Syrian rue); and the Near East produced the tree of knowledge, the pomegranate. Nor were ancient physicians unaware of the psychedelic effects of

---

What They Nibble with Their Tea in the East

A favorite Oriental accompaniment to tea is pistachio nuts—often in great quantities. In some areas, pomegranate seeds are chewed.

Warning: If pistachios happen to be your passion, make sure you buy organic ones in a health food store, because nut products can be heavily laced with a fungal poison called aflatoxin. In some tests conducted in 1998 the German government found that pistachios exceeded acceptable levels of this toxin to a spectacular degree: they contained eighteen times more than the maximum levels allowed in Germany! Those nuts happened to come from Iran, but care should be taken with nuts imported from other countries too because fungal toxins can damage human DNA and cause cancer. The source of the poison is a mold that can invade any product which is not manufactured or stored correctly.

mandrake, wormwood and banewort (*Atropa belladonna*). They were all made to serve the sexual appetite. That is why the poppy came to be called the "bliss plant."

The earliest evidence of aphrodisiac potions is in papyrus texts from ancient Egypt. The doctors of that time used the same standbys we use today: hemp, opium, thornapple and a series of stimulating spices. Many of these ancient recipes are employed to this day, as, for example, the Oriental Happiness Pill.

Of the plants treated in this book, the ones with a reputation for stimulating the sexual urge are: anise, basil, stinging nettle, vervain, *damiana*, thornapple (datura), galangal or Siamese ginger, pomegranate, ginger, cardamom, coriander, ephedra (sometimes called sea grape), allspice, rosemary, yarrow, celery, tea shrub, grains, wormwood and cinnamon.

Damiana Tea

3 parts dried damiana
2 parts dried peppermint
bitter orange blossoms

Mix the herbs and cover with boiling water. Let steep 5 minutes.

Arabian Jasmine Water

Cover a handful of Arabian jasmine flowers (see the list of suppliers at the back of the book) with cold water and allow to steep for a few hours or overnight. This makes an exquisite drink for the enchanted hours of love.

Ephedra or Sea Grape Tea

Bring to a boil 1 or 2 heaped tablespoons of dried ephedra per cup of tea and steep for 10 minutes. Add a pinch of anise and some dried mint and allow to steep for a few more minutes. Strain and sweeten to taste.

The sexual stimulation begins to take effect after a quarter of an hour. In making this tea for men, caution is advised: an overdose will have the opposite effect from the one desired.

There Are Other Ways to Enjoy Tea

One of the secondary tools of Oriental health management was the *hammam*, the public bath. We know today that this traditional hygienic institution was of great importance.

The *hammam* was equipped with hot and cold baths, steam baths and trained masseurs. It did a lot to promote the health and natural resistance of its regular visitors. The physical experience and the sensuous atmosphere of the *hammam* could enhance sexual performance, too.

The Bath for 1001 Nights

2 oz. (50 g) rose petals
1 oz. (20 g) peppermint leaves
3 drops essence of rose or rose geranium
a little honey

Enclose the dry ingredients in a little bag and tie it shut. Run some very hot water over the bag as you fill the tub. Meanwhile, stir the essential oils with the honey and add them to the bath. While you are bathing, give the bag of herbs a squeeze every now and then. Sip a herbal tea of your choice while you are soaking. This bath is soothing and calming, and it loosens the muscles.

Bathe Like the Queen of Sheba

For a tub bath you will need to mix well: ½ l milk, ¼ l cream, 3–4 tablespoons of fluid honey, and a few drops of some of your best-loved essential oils, for example:

Pharaoh Mixture:
5 drops sandalwood oil
5 drops oil of bergamot
2 drops oil of cardamom
5 drops geranium oil
2 drops coriander oil

1 drop oil of pepper

Strew 2 or 3 handfuls of rose petals over the surface of the water. Quickly pull the phone out of the wall, turn off the doorbell and lock the bathroom door, so that you can really enjoy your magic Oriental bath. Quiet music and a good tea will round out the experience. Do nothing, think nothing, be nothing …

Now Maybe You Would Like a Relaxing Massage?

For a massage oil, prepare the following recipe:

Oriental Bouquet:
8 drops sandalwood oil

3 drops oil of vetiver
1 drop vanilla oil
5 drops oil of patchouli
2 drops Peruvian balsam oil
1 drop oil of cardamom
15-20 drops of almond oil

And With It a Rose Tea

Make your usual black tea and add a handful of fresh, fragrant rose petals to the cup. Let it steep a bit and enjoy it. This tea is a joy to look at. It is possible to buy rose tea already prepared.

So That the Swoon of Love Will Have No Consequences ...

Some information has come down to us about Oriental methods of contraception. In the Papyrus Ebers we read: "So that a woman does not become pregnant for one, two or three years: Mix finely ground leaves of the Egyptian thorn acacia, colocynth [colocynth apples or bitter gourd] and dates with a bit of honey. Put this mixture together with cotton threads into her vagina." Crocodile dung was another substance that was pressed together with plant parts and—using the thick, sticky juice of other plants—made into tampons. In Cleopatra's time, women are known to have poured oil of cedar into the vagina. There are also reports about vaginal suppositories made of pine bark and wine.

The pomegranate is the most interesting of the ancient methods of contraception. This fruit contains large amounts of plant estrogen, which is supposed to resemble very closely the female sexual hormone. It is possible to assume, therefore, that it will exert a similar effect inside a woman's body. With experience and the careful use of the precious fruit, it is possible that women could exercise some control over their conceptions. The preparation of the contraceptive was relatively simple: the crushed pomegranate seeds were rolled in wax and used as a vaginal suppository. But the drink made of pomegranates was probably more effective: the seeds were crushed and washed down with water. In Oriental countries we still encounter many women who seem to be chewing pomegranate seeds all day.

Although we are not quite sure how they worked, these recipes must have been at least partially effective. If not efficient as a barrier to semen, the various plant materials would no doubt have influenced the chemical environment offered to the semen by the vagina. For example, it has been shown that the leaves of the acacia tree will produce lactic acid when they ferment; in this way they can put the semen out of action, rendering it a harmless visitor.

THE AMERICAS

FATHER SUN, MOTHER EARTH
HEALING WAYS OF THE NATIVE PEOPLE

At a time when no one in Europe even dreamed of continents across the Atlantic, numerous civilizations developed, flourished and decayed in the Americas. For Europeans, America only started to exist when Columbus "discovered" it, in the course of his search for India. And indeed he believed he had arrived at his goal and regarded the Native people he encountered as "Indians." In the "New World" the Europeans found large city states with complex infrastructures, including good hospitals. In the Andes the mighty empire of the Incas flourished. Plant collectors, traders and huntsmen roamed the deserts and rain forests, commuted between tribes and families, and moved between heaven and earth. They were in intimate alignment with nature and had mastered many of her own strategies of survival.

The largest city state in the Americas was in Mexico—Tenochtitlán, the center of Aztec civilization. The ruler of the Aztecs, Montezuma II (1502-20) owned a botanical garden. In it, a host of gardeners tended about four thousand plants, most of them used for healing. Ready-made plant preparations, such as healing juices, salves and poultices, were sold in pharmacies around the city.

Very much like the Chinese, who base their medicine on the balance of Yin and Yang, the South and Central American Aboriginal peoples view all manifestations as expressions of opposing and complementary forces that normally maintain a state of equilibrium. Masculine energy requires the feminine; Mother Earth has to have Father Sun. This is an insight that even contemporary science can no longer deny. Clearly, without Father Sun there would be no life on Mother Earth. When the harmony of the complementary forces is disturbed, human beings fall ill.

The healing ceremonies of Native medicine therefore aim at restoring harmony. Their herbs, which are very efficacious, are regarded as useful components of the central ritual. All plants with healing powers are seen as a gift of the gods and are worshiped accordingly. Some are even regarded as teachers and treated with special reverence.

The Aztecs held their medical lore in common with many other tribes and peoples of Central America and Mexico. Unfortunately, the conquistadores destroyed numerous New World cultures. Yet the healing power of the native herbs never failed to amaze them, especially the physicians that traveled with the troops.

Aztec medicine made a particularly strong impression on the Spanish. Phillip II, the king of Spain, sent his personal physician to South America to study Aztec healing. This doctor worked in Mexico for several years, collecting medical information that he eventually brought back to his own country. This early intellectual "export" has turned out to be far more important than all the treasure the Spanish took back with them. Of course, among those exported plants were the potato, the tomato and chocolate, as well as the original ingredients of the pill—and where would our culture be without these things?

The Inca empire too had developed a notable body of medical knowledge. Both the physician and the pharmacist were established professionals. Herbs from the Amazon Delta and the rain forests were traded briskly all over the

Cacti and tree bark were used by the Aztecs and Incas to produce effective curatives, which have attracted the attention of researchers. The best examples: maté and Lapacho tea. (Also see the picture on pp. 86–7.)

country. Their extensive network of trade routes—parts of which are still in use today—connected Aboriginal peoples of different cultures. This ensured that, despite differences in language and customs, the indigenous peoples shared a common body of medical knowledge and set of treatment modalities.

The good news about the amazing medicinal powers of American plants spread across Europe very quickly. By the beginning of the nineteenth century, arrowroot, chili, jalapeno root, cornsilk, cinnamon bark, balsam of Peru, sarsaparilla and sassafras were all known as common household remedies. Many important drugs were discovered in the course of pharmacological research into the healing powers of American plants, and they are still used by doctors today for local anesthesia, to treat psychological illnesses or as aids in the treatment of heart conditions. Homeopathy too was the result of this type of research: Samuel Hahnemann, who developed this healing mode, was actually experimenting with cinchona bark when he discovered that you could cure "like with like." American plants make up a large part of the pharmacopoeia of homeopathy, and almost all the plants discussed in this book can be found in the form of homeopathic tinctures.

All the research has revealed that for centuries past the Aboriginal peoples of the western hemisphere have been practicing medicine with great sensitivity and deep insight. While Europeans were mocking their primitive, holistic view of nature, the Indians were actually light-years ahead of European medicine. For one thing, no Native family is a stranger to the use of healing herbs, and the treatment of any condition begins at home. Only when all home remedies fail will a professional be called in, be it doctor, pharmacist, medicine man or woman, shaman or midwife. Among the most common home remedies are: chili pepper, coca leaves, guarana, cocoa, potato, pumpkin seeds, corn, maté, Mormon tea, papaya, arrowroot, allspice, sunflower seeds, tomato and vanilla.

The Native healers also received into their repertoire many new plants imported by the conquistadores, namely, dandelion, wild chicory, bindweed, mustard, coriander, wormwood, sage, fennel, St. John's wort, peppermint, mallow, rue and sorrel. Most of the herbs described in the following section are readily available in drugstores or health food stores, and in most cases their medicinal powers have been recognized.

Most American tribes use healing herbs primarily in the form of teas. Herbal decoctions are also prepared to soothe or cure various ailments. Poultices are known, but in marked contrast to Egyptian medicine, very few salves are made or used. As a rule the freshest herbs are selected, placed in cold water and brought to a boil. The brew is then allowed to steep. Plants are practically never steeped in cold water to make an extract, probably because cold water is not germ-free and could cause complications. Many Amerindians regard smoking certain intoxicating or healing plants as therapeutic. Acute pain, for example, is much easier to bear with the help of analgesic smoke. Smoking can also deliver a healing expansion of consciousness. In South America healing plants are frequently chewed. Great significance is also assigned to the benefits of enemas, as the Indians are convinced that the intestines and digestion are critical to human health.

The Essential Herbs of the Aboriginal Peoples of the Americas

The plants chosen for inclusion in this chapter are to a greater or lesser extent known to and used by all the different Native peoples of the Americas. They are all described together for the sake of clarity. In the selection we also took into account their availability to readers of this book. Recipes featuring the specific plants described in this section are given immediately after the description of each plant.

Californian Buckthorn

Rhamnus purshiana The bark of this tree served the Indians as laxative and purge. They called it "sacred bark" and, before preparing the healing decoction, they let the bark rest for at least a year. Today we know that storing the bark for a long time does indeed increase its efficacy. Buckthorn bark also works against pain if it is chewed slowly. Recent scientific research has established that the tea made of the bark strengthens the immune system.

This species of buckthorn is also known as cascara sagrada. It can be obtained in herbal or health food stores. The correct dosage seems to be ½ teaspoon of the bark to 1 cup of hot water, steeped for 10 to 15 minutes, then strained. You can drink one fresh cup of this tea in the morning and evening. Tea of cascara sagrada, however, should not be taken at all without first consulting a physician, and even then not for a prolonged period. Supplements consisting largely of *Rhamnus purshiana* are also available.

Avocado

Persea americana The avocado is one of the oldest fruits known to man. Its name derives from the Aztec word *auacatl*. While the fruit itself was eaten, the rest of the plant had medici-

nal and contraceptive uses. The Maya tie avocado leaves to the soles of the feet of fever patients; against a cough, a tea is brewed from the tender shoots of the tree. The Indians of Paraguay prevent conception with a decoction of avocado.

Avocado Helps against Diarrhea

Split and grate an avocado stone and roast the ground nut meat in a pan. Bring to a boil in a cup of water with 1 teaspoon ribwort leaves (*Plantago lanceolata*). Steep a short time and strain.

Boldo

Peumus boldus Originally a native of Chile, the boldo tree is now established all through Central America and Mexico as well. The tree's foliage gives off a scent reminiscent of a mixture of camphor and peppermint. Boldo leaves have many uses in Native medicine, for example against worms and diarrhea. Mixed with horsetail (*Equisetum*) boldo leaves furnish a general healing tea. Boldo is also esteemed as a remedy against every sort of uterine dysfunction. A tea made of the plant is often served after meals to further the digestion. Boldo leaves constitute one of the most common remedies in Central and South America and are also readily available outside those regions.

Boldo Tea

Bring 0.1 oz. (4 g) leaves of boldo tree to a boil in 2 cups (500 ml) water with some honey. Steep the tea for 2 days. A cup should be drunk in the morning on an empty stomach, and another cup in the evening. Placing the container in the open air when the moon is full is said to give the tea more power.

Boldo tea is recommended in various situations: anxiety attacks, nervous depression, loss of appetite (drink the tea *before* meals!) and digestive difficulties.

Chili Pepper

Capsicum frutescens Chilies belong to the botanical family of the nightshades. The small red peppers are close relatives of the green and red peppers we eat in salads. There are actually about seventy different varieties of chilies. In the Americas chilies have been eaten as far back as memory goes. The Spanish brought chilies to Europe. Along with pepper, ginger and turmeric, chilies are now the most-used spice worldwide. Chili peppers constitute an extraordinarily effective source of energy; they promote digestion and awaken sensuality.

Chili Pepper Tea
Make your favorite herbal tea and sweeten it with honey. Add a tiny pinch of chili pepper, stir well and drink in small sips, as warm as you can. This will help with fevers, weak metabolism—and shyness!

Cinchona Tree

Cinchona pubescens The cinchona tree has given us quinine, which is used with good effect against malaria and other fevers. The Aboriginal peoples of South America prepared a healing potion from the bark of the tree to administer to fever patients. Its effectiveness became the stuff of legends. We know that it was the Jesuits who brought cinchona bark to Europe in the year 1642. Although the healing effect of the drug was well known and acknowledged in Protestant countries, it was not taken seriously at first, and in some places was even banned, because it was known as "the bark of the satanic papists." Later in the history of medicine, Peruvian bark, as it was also called, became available in powder form at pharmacies and was consumed as tea. Eventually, the drug acquired serious economic importance. Its components, chinine and chinidine, are found in many contemporary medicines. Tonic water too contains extract of cinchona bark.

The Native peoples of Central America and Mexico cooked a tea of cinchona bark. A tablespoon of the chopped bark, which is available in herbal stores, was steeped in 2 cups (500 ml) boiling water. A patient suffering from fever was given a cup of this tea several times a day. It is also possible to make a wine with the plant: To 1 l dry white wine add 2 tablespoons of the dry bark of cinchona tree. Let it stand for 5 days and spice it a bit to mask the bitterness, perhaps with a little cinnamon or saffron. It is quite possible to overdose on cinchona, so consult a doctor before you start using either the tea or the wine.

Condurango or Eagle Vine

Marsdenia cundurango This liana is named after the condor, a large South American bird believed by the Indians to have been blessed by the gods with many extraordinary faculties. Indeed, decoctions of this climbing plant have been used by Native healers against a range of syndromes, stomach ailments, nervous conditions, tumors and venereal diseases.

Condurango Wine
If you suffer from difficulties of the digestive tract, feel overfull or have no appetite, reach for your condurango wine, which you make by

adding a handful of eagle vine bark chips to a bottle of heavy, sweet wine, such as port or Madeira. The bark can be bought from a herbalist. You must allow the infusion to steep for five days before drinking it, however, since the active ingredients dissolve only gradually, in cold liquids. Drink a small glass before meals. Do not take this remedy for long, as you can overdose on condurango. To make an alcohol-free tea, add ½ teaspoon condurango per cup to the amount of water you need and bring to a boil. Let the tea cool off before drinking it.

Damiana

Turnera diffusa or aphrodisiaca Our name for the plant derives from that of the Spanish missionary Saint Damian, patron of pharmacists. The Aztecs were more explicit about the aphrodisiac powers of the plant in calling it "the one that tears the shirt off a man's back." Damiana continues to be an important plant in the pharmacopoeia of the Aboriginal peoples. It is valuable as a tonic and nerve stimulant. The Indians took damiana when they were exhausted. With respiratory diseases the plant acts as a "broom for the bronchial tubes."

Enlivening Damiana Tea
You can buy dried damiana leaves from any good herbalist. (See also the list of suppliers at the end of this book.)

> *3 parts dried damiana*
> *2 parts dried peppermint leaves*
> *1 part orange blossoms*

For a cup of this tea, brew 1 tablespoon of the mixture with boiling water and let sit for 5 min-

utes before straining. Sweeten with honey and drink in small sips, as you feel the need.

Against PMS or Pain
Pour 1 cup (250 ml) boiling water over 1 tablespoon of damiana leaves and allow to steep for 5 to 10 minutes. The longer the tea sits, the more effective it becomes. Drink a cup of this tea several times a day.

The ethnopharmacologist Christian Rätsch shares this Mayan recipe, for which the ingredients can be found at any health food or herb store. Mix well 1 measure each of buckthorn (*Rhamnus cathartica*), mallow, rosemary, laurel and anise with 3 measures of damiana. From this mixture take 1 tablespoon per cup of boiling water and let the tea steep for 5 minutes. This

tea, which soothes both the stomach and the intestines, tastes good, too.

When you have a cold, you can boil damiana petals and either add the strained liquid to your bath or use the still-steaming pot for an inhalation. Occasionally, damiana can be added to any tea, to stimulate the heart or the metabolism—or for its erotic powers.

Angel's Trumpet or Tree Datura

Brugmansia candida Since time immemorial the Native peoples have known of the intoxicating gift of the beautiful angel's trumpet. They prepare from it a drink they call *tonga*. Today they smoke both the leaves and the blossoms, to clear up respiratory disorders and as an aphrodisiac. Teas and decoctions are also employed. The use of tree datura is dangerous: an overdose leads to respiratory arrest. So be warned! It is possible to benefit from the eroticizing powers of the plant by sitting under it on a hot summer evening and breathing in its intoxicating scent. Angel's trumpet is available for your terrace or balcony as a container plant.

Cocoa

See Chocolate on page 99.

Coca Shrub

Erythroxylon coca Although we can no longer brew a tea from coca leaves, the plant is included here for the sake of completeness, as it has great importance for us as well as for the Aboriginal peoples. In the empire of the Incas the coca shrub was sacred. Its leaves served mostly ritual and ceremonial purposes. Ethnopharmacologists tell us that before a man could participate in the coca harvest, he had to

have slept with a woman; this ensured that divine Mother Coca would feel satisfied. To prolong the act of love a man's penis would be rubbed with a decoction of coca leaves. Later, coca leaves were used to anesthetize patients during operations. The plant was considered a heal-all. Fresh leaves made into tea were administered to stop colic. It is said that, sweetened with brown sugar, this same tea is effective against stomach ache, diarrhea, sore throat, headache, fever and rheumatism.

In the sixteenth century the active ingredient, cocaine, was extracted. It took another two hundred years before this substance was submitted to pharmacological analysis. Then as now, cocaine was abused as a stimulating drug, and it is by no means free of side effects. From the start, scientists have tried to find medical uses for the powers of the plant and now have a long list of healing and sedative medications to show for it. And of course we all use Coca Cola and salty pretzels to settle our stomach, stop the runs, and counteract nausea and seasickness when we travel.

Cat's Claw

Uncaria tomentosa Cat's claw is a rain forest climber. It is not known what purpose the plant served among the Native people. (I think this plant is new to most botanists. I looked at standard works and at books on rain forest plants and found no trace of *Uncaria tomentosa*.) European scientists have studied the effects of Cat's claw in fighting cancer, and have found the results promising. The chemicals present in the "thorn claw" strengthen the immune system and stimulate the body's powers of self-regeneration. Tea of thorn claw can be bought

in some health food stores, but it is expensive because the plant is very rare.

Corn
Zea mays For over ten thousand years corn has been the most important staple in the Mexican diet. Although we have adopted corn into our kitchens, we know little about the plant's healing properties. The Maya feed their sick with nothing but corn. A patient who rejects corn is considered at death's door. A tea made of cornsilk is used all over Central America and Mexico as a universal remedy against constipation, diarrhea, infertility and menstrual difficulties. Japanese and Chinese doctors have discovered that corn will lower blood sugar levels and helps in regulating blood pressure. It may be possible to buy cornsilk in your health food or herbal store.

Purifying Cornsilk Tea
Cook 2 oz. (50 g) dried cornsilk in 4 cups (1 l) water for 10 minutes. Drinking 2 or 3 cups a day will regulate your blood pressure. It also helps with bladder inflammations.

Maté
Ilex paraguariensis See page 104.

Mormon Tea
Ephedra americana Mormon Tea is a mixture of several varieties of ephedra. It is also known as Indian Tea. A decoction of the roots is prepared. It is supposed to work against venereal disease, rheumatism, bladder inflammations and gallbladder irritation. Ephedra and its active ingredient, ephedrine, are acknowledged medicinal substances. Since ephedra is only available on prescription, this tea has to be bought in a pharmacy. Allow 1 teaspoon per cup of boiling water and let steep for 10 minutes. An overdose of ephedra can cause nervousness and even heart problems. Before you start using it, consult your physician.

Evening Primrose
Oenothera biennis In Peru evening primrose is held in particularly high regard as an effective healing plant. The Indians of that country use it to regulate the menses and against fever, headache, stomach upset and contusions. In the last few years primrose oil has been recommended for premenstrual syndrome. This oil is rare and valuable because it promotes the production of the hormone prostaglandin. It is supposed to be helpful in all cases of weakness. It is available in capsule form in health food and drug stores.

Papaya
Carica papaya Among the commonly available exotic fruits, papaya stands out as a real healing champion. Not only does it taste delicious, but it also has a multiplicity of positive effects on the body. Papaya improves digestion, calms the stomach and frees the intestines of worms. The fruit also contains papain, an enzyme that splits protein molecules and deconstructs dead cell material, thereby detoxifying the body. Furthermore, papaya is rich in vitamins. Since 1552 papaya leaves have been used in Europe for healing and continue to be sold at most local health food stores.

Papaya Leaf Tea
Pour boiling water over 1 teaspoon papaya leaves and allow to sit for about 20 minutes.

Indian healers use this tea with asthma patients. It is also worth investigating supplements that contain the enzyme papain.

Passion Flower

Passiflora incarnata This beautiful climber is available in nurseries in North America and Europe. The plant received its name from missionaries, who saw in it the Cross and all other symbols of the Passion of Christ. The Native people of the Andes used the passion flower in cases of constipation and even with arrest of peristalsis, and also against nervous tension and low spirits. It is said that the plant bestows good dreams. The Indians and the Spanish love to slurp the juicy pulp of the passion fruit itself.

Dried passion flower can be obtained in any herbal store. Do not attempt to use the leaves of your ornamental plant to make tea, however, as this plant is a cultivar with different qualities. It is also said that tea of passion flower is not as effective as the extract, sold in capsules.

Allspice

Pimenta dioia We know the plant as a spice under various names: allspice, pimento or Jamaica pepper. The *Pimenta* tree, a member of the family of *myrtaceae*, is a small evergreen that grows in Central and South America and in India. The fragrance of its fruit reminds one of cloves, nutmeg, pepper and cinnamon. The ancient Maya used to chew the leaves when they had toothache, a digestive disorder or loss of appetite. As a preventive measure against colds, allspice powder can be mixed with cocoa and sweetened with honey.

Allspice Drink for Stomach Ache
Add a small pinch of freshly ground allspice to a glass of warm milk and sweeten it with honey. You can drink 2 glasses a day.

Ratanhia

Krameria triandra In Peru, ratanhia is still frequently used against inflammations of the gums and bladder. The plant has anti-inflammatory and styptic powers. Ratanhia root can be obtained in herbal stores. For a tea, about 0.1 oz. (2 g) per cup are simmered for about 10 minutes. You can also use the tea as a gargle. You may be able to buy a prepared tea that contains ratanhia.

Sage

Salvia Sage is regarded as one of the most significant plants by the North and South American Aboriginal people, as they use it for healing and ceremonial purposes. Sage smoke is said to be a spiritual purifier, releasing inspiration and creating inner clarity. Medically speaking, sage is useful with colds and all diseases of the mouth and throat. The plant has proved itself with healers of both the American and European traditions, but the South American species of *Salvia* are incomparably more powerful. The sage used by the Aztecs is available from herbalists, as are other species. It is easy to obtain various ready-made sage teas.

Ancient Native herbal formulas, such as the "Original Indian Essence," said to be the life elixir of Amerindians, were treasured by European healers as important medical secrets. In the background is the medicine wheel.

98

Sage Tea for Anxiety Attacks

In milder cases of panic and stress, Indian healers rely on the calming virtues of sage. Bring 1 ½ oz. (4 g) dry sage leaves to a boil with 2 cups (500 ml) water, allow to steep for a short time and strain. One cup, morning and evening, over a number of days should relieve the angst.

Sarsaparilla

Smilax regelii Aztec doctors used sarsaparilla and nowadays the tea made from this plant is consumed to counteract all manner of complaints, from pimples to venereal disease and fever. Science supports the power of sarsaparilla as a diuretic and diaphoretic, as well as in clearing the complexion. Root of sarsaparilla can be bought in a heath food store or from a herbalist.

Cold Water Infusion for Pimples
5 parts sarsaparilla root
2 parts strawberry leaves
2 parts blackberry (bramble) leaves
1 part cinchona bark

Place all ingredients in cold water and allow to steep overnight. Drink as required. According to the latest research, sarsaparilla also works against psoriasis.

Amerindian medicine employs the following simple sarsaparilla tea against bladder infections and pains: Pour boiling water over 1 teaspoon chopped, dried sarsaparilla root and set aside for a short time. Strain and drink the hot liquid slowly. You can take several cups of freshly made tea over the course of the day.

Sassafras Tree

Sassafras albidum The Aboriginal peoples of the Americas count the sassafras tree among their sacred plants. In addition to its spiritual significance, the tree also has value as a healing plant. Root, bark, leaves and berries are all processed into an assortment of teas, which are variously used against rheumatism, venereal disease, cough, bladder disorders and jitteriness. Plant parts are also put into poultices for wounds, broken bones and contusions. Moreover, the sassafras is considered a very effective aphrodisiac. The fragrance of the plant is reminiscent of orange, lemon and vanilla.

The Spanish are responsible for bringing the plant to Europe in the sixteenth century. The bark soon gained a reputation as a medicinal substance. It is available in health food stores and lends itself well to herbal combinations. Your herbalist may have some suggestions in this regard.

Yarrow

Achillea millefolium This plant, which is native to both Europe and the Americas, was a standby of Aztec doctors. To this day, tea of yarrow is given to people who suffer from mood swings. It is also said to help with the symptoms of menstruation, tuberculosis, hemorrhoids, diarrhea, colds and toothache. Actually, science has confirmed most of these uses of the plant. Yarrow is readily available in health food stores.

Yarrow as an All-round Tea

Pour 1 cup (250 ml) boiling water over 2 teaspoons of the herb and strain after it has steeped for about 10 minutes. You can drink as many as 3 or 4 cups a day, if desired. This tea can

be sweetened with honey and flavored with mint leaves or anise.

The ethno-pharmacologist Christian Rätsch recommends another yarrow tea of Amerindian origin, which is helpful with rheumatic complaints, achy limbs and loss of appetite.

3 parts yarrow
2 parts damiana
1 part willow bark
1 part calamus or sweet flag root (Acorus calamus*)*

For 1 cup, take 1 teaspoon of this mixture, pour boiling water over it, let sit for 5 to 10 minutes and drink warm.

Chocolate

Theobroma cacao Tchocolatl is the name the Aztecs gave to the spice they made from the bean-shaped seeds of the cocoa tree. This tree's native habitat extended over the regions of the Amazon and Orinoco rivers. The Aztecs enjoyed cocoa as a source of energy and good spirits. They also appreciated its diuretic effects. Powdered cocoa is won from the beans by a process of fermentation, roasting and grinding. It is a spice in the cuisines of South America, Spain and Italy. Chocolate, however, was invented in Europe. The chemicals contained in chocolate resemble those that the body produces when a person is in love. This explains why people with emotional troubles or depression seek consolation in chocolate. The only reason chocolate is never given credit for these great qualities is that it is also high in sugar and calories.

Hot chocolate made of real cocoa shells (buy them in the health food store) helps against diarrhea, exhaustion, loss of energy and loss of your partner. Take 1 teaspoon of cocoa shell, pour 1 cup (250 ml) boiling water over it and let it steep for 5 to 10 minutes. It is important to use real cocoa shell, not the prepared cocoa powder sold in supermarkets, which will have hardly any effect at all. Real cocoa shell tea is available to buy from Schoenenberger and Salus (Cacaohülsentee). For an energizing tea you can bring cocoa powder to a boil with milk. Add a pinch of anise and chili pepper, a pod of vanilla, a stick of cinnamon, a few chopped nuts and some arrowroot powder. After you have strained it, you can sweeten this tea with brown sugar.

Here is another chocolate recipe the Amerindians use to improve their spirits:

1 cup (250 ml) fresh whole milk
1 vanilla pod
2 tablespoons real cocoa powder
1 pinch chili pepper
1 pinch salt
1 tablespoon honey

Bring the milk to a boil, lower the heat, add the vanilla pod and simmer very gently for 5 to 10 minutes. Take out the vanilla pod and scratch out the black seeds, putting them in a bowl or cup. Add the spices and cocoa and a little of the milk and whip with a wire whisk until completely dissolved. Return to the pot, add the remaining milk, stir well and reheat without boiling. Serve hot.

Echinacea or Coneflower

Echinacea angustifolia This flower has become very famous in the last few years. Its medicinal properties have been known to pharmacologists for some years, but now a new industry has grown around its cultivation and distribution. Indian tribal healers applied echinacea in a variety of different medical situations, namely, in dressing wounds, against inflammations, as an antidote to certain poisons and to strengthen general resistance. At this time echinacea is one of the most effective natural ways to stabilize the immune system. Echinacea supplements are available and are considered more effective than homemade teas.

Echinacea Tea for Better Overall Fitness
Use 1 heaping tablespoon of the herb per cup of tea. Boil the water in an enamel, glass or stainless steel pot—not aluminum—and pour over the plant parts. Let this tea sit for 10 minutes. Strain and drink in small sips; it can be enjoyed cold or hot.

Vanilla
Vanilla planifolia This popular and expensive spice is a member of the orchid family and originated in Mexico. The Aztecs valued the vanilla pod; they offered it on festive occasions and gave it to their rulers to show them deference. One of the Spanish conquerors reported in 1520 that Montezuma was served a drink made of chocolate and vanilla—allegedly to prepare him for amorous adventures. It is not impossible, however, that the king was given this drink to counteract "Montezuma's vengeance," since chocolate was, and still is, used as a reliable remedy for diarrhea.

The Maya appreciate the power of vanilla to this day, and drink a tea made of vanilla pods, peppermint leaves and the fruit of balsam of Peru, to strengthen the heart when they suffer from sexual exhaustion. Central and South American Aboriginal peoples generally attribute a mild aphrodisiac effect to vanilla and they hold the plant in high regard. Try to buy real vanilla whenever possible. Most of the vanilla extract that is sold is artificial. Vanilla tea is available in some health food stores.

Vanilla Drink
Simmer a cup of milk with 1 teaspoon dried, chopped vanilla pod, drain and drink. You can also add some honey, cocoa and arrowroot powder.

Willow
Salix We can thank the willow for one of our most beloved, most used, most useful and most successful medicines: aspirin. New benefits of aspirin are continually being discovered. At first it was used only against pain and inflammation. Now it is considered an important way to prevent heart and circulatory diseases.

Many Aboriginal tribes prepare a decoction of willow bark against headaches, sore limbs and rheumatic complaints. The decoction is also effective against cold and flu. A tea made of willow bark will lower fever, alleviate pain and relieve rheumatic symptoms. Willow bark can be obtained from a health food store or herbalist.

Willow Tea
Place 1 tablespoon of willow bark per cup into a teapot and pour in the required amount of boiling water. Let this steep for 15 to 20 minutes. Use this tea only to cure your complaint; do not drink willow bark tea for long periods of time. To make a decoction, place the willow bark in cold water, bring to a boil and simmer for 10 minutes. The decoction is supposed to be more efficient.

Rare Herbs and Tea Recipes from the Rain Forest

We are fascinated by the rain forest, which is green and lush all year. The people who live there receive all they need from the forest: food, medicine, shelter—their very basis of existence. The Native people of the rain forest learn from early childhood how to treat small cuts and gashes and what works during mild episodes of ill health. The plants they learn to administer in the small crises of daily life grow in the immediate vicinity of their homes: chili pepper, allspice, cocoa, tea, avocado, cinnamon, sweet galingale, clove, nutmeg and papaya.

Severe illnesses are treated by experienced healers, shamans or magicians. In reaching a diagnosis these experts are likely to include dreams and dream interpretations in their professional tool kit. Among the rain forest shamans known for their healing arts are magicians, soothsayers and fetish priests. Then there are the herbalists, who command an extensive knowledge of the healing properties of plants. Midwives are called in to deal with all matters relating to the female realm, among them menstruation, pregnancy, birth and contraception. Their repertoire includes plants, rituals and magical procedures, but they also dispense advice and stand by women in need.

The inhabitants of the rain forest live in two worlds: the visible world and an invisible one. The latter is called the "true reality," the "reality of the soul," or the "invisible world." This reality is both within man and the basis for all existence outside him. This reality is a place of dreams. It is beyond the gods and goddesses, whose living breath fills and enlivens all that thrives within the forest. To reach this inner world and to expand one's consciousness, plants with psychoactive powers are brought into play. They are called master plants and plant teachers.

Ayahuasca—Amazon Magic

For the Native people of the rain forest the most important means of reaching the other world is via a magic potion made from the climber ayahuasca (*Banisteriopsis caapi*). Many visitors to the rain forest—including doctors and missionaries—report incredible experiences after imbibing this magic drink. The potion heightens the telepathic powers of the user. Scientists have analyzed the secrets of this magical liana, inasmuch as that can be done. Actually, ayahuasca does not bear sole responsibility for the extraordinary effects of the potion; as a rule, chacruna is also added. The chemical substances in these plants—the souls of the two plants—complement each other in such a way that they can facilitate a trip into the "real world." The shamans of the Amazon tribes regard the judicious use of ayahuasca as one of the mainstays of their profession. When a particular disease is diagnosed, other healing herbs are combined with ayahuasca. Often the potion will induce forceful vomiting and diarrhea in the patient, thus ridding her body of the causes of the illness.

How the potion is prepared used to be a well-guarded secret. Today this mystery of the rain forest has been analyzed and patented in the United States. What may appear as progress at first glance is really a violation of the rights of those who have preserved the secret of this powerful remedy. In the future they will be able to administer this potion—a part of their own, ancient cultural heritage—only after paying a hefty licensing fee to the owners of the patent. The process will also kill the souls of the plants involved.

We can thank the healers of the primeval forest for many good drugs. Curare, the poison used on arrows, has been chemically analyzed, and the drugs that have been created from its components include anesthetics, muscle relaxants and various cramp-releasing remedies that modern medicine has come to rely on. The destruction of the rain forests and of the peoples and cultures it nourishes robs us of the chance for further valuable medical insights. It also erases the native habitat of all sorts of plants, foods and spices that we have come to love, such as cocoa, vanilla, cinnamon, banana, avocado, papaya and mango.

There are many rain forest plants that serve as components in our own medicines: araroba tree, peanut, paprika, ipecacuanha, coca shrub, cotton, lignum vitae (*Guaiacum*), manioc, condurango shrub, balsam tree, devil pepper (*Rauwolfia apcynaceae*), cocoa tree, real vanilla and corn. To the degree that a plant of the rain forest can be made into a tea, it has been described in this chapter.

Something Extraordinary—CoD Rainforest Tea

The shamans of the rain forest are able to heal diseases for which we have no cure—or so we are told. Thomas David, a physician, undertook extensive treks through the rain forest in search of unknown remedies. He has learned what plants and teas will strengthen the immune system so effectively that the body is able to defend and heal itself even under attack from the most severe illnesses. On his return he and his team of researchers tested various teas on patients who had been written off by modern medicine. He reports that they were able to improve the quality of life for all patients, after they were put on tailor-made diets and given teas to fit their condition. Even people who were completely depleted after radical surgery reacted well to the treatment based on supporting their own healing abilities.

Today, Thomas David can offer his CoD Rainforest Tea, consisting of several herbs, in Canada and the United States. (See list of addresses at the end of the book.) The prolonged curative use of the tea, however, should not be attempted without consulting a physician. Nor can this tea replace the methods of Western medicine. Thomas David himself has said: "Notwithstanding our many positive results, I would never be so bold as to claim that our phyto-therapeutic system can cure cancer." According to his experience, however, an improvement in the general condition of patients takes place almost invariably.

Guarana—A Hit with the Kids

The peoples of the Amazon have known for thousands of years that guarana (*Paullinia cupana*) will stimulate mental and physical strength, counteract fatigue, and alleviate sensations of hunger and thirst. In hot and humid weather it is a useful source of extra energy. Guarana tea is taken for migraine, depression due to PMS, and diarrhea, and as an aphrodisiac. Guarana is freely available, as a powder or in pill form, and is often sold in nightclubs and fitness centers. Caution is indicated with the use of this drug, and its critics claim that you can achieve the same high by drinking an espresso.

The plants and fruits of the rain forest offer a cornucopia of colors and tastes: cocoa, wild papaya, aloe, orchid, fern and pineapple.

Unique Herbs and Healing Teas from the High Andes

Yerba Maté, the Green Gold of the Indios

Yerba Maté is the elixir of life for the inhabitants of the high Andes. The cultivation of Yerba maté began in South America thousands of years ago. It is assumed that the Native people of South America routinely chewed packets of Yerba maté and coca leaves. Today Yerba maté is enjoyed mostly in the form of tea; it has become the national drink of several South American countries. It is offered to welcome each visitor. The tea ceremony proceeds at a leisurely pace. Peace and calm reign. Medicinally, the tea is used to treat all sorts of complaints, often augmented by other herbs.

Tea made of Yerba maté is called the green gold of the Aboriginal people. It is said to contribute to their proverbial vitality and physical stamina. The leaves of the evergreen shrub (*Ilex paraguariensis*) have been made into a stimulating and vitamin-rich tea since ancient times. We call this tea Yerba maté, but to the Native people *mati* refers to the small bottle gourd from which the tea is drunk with a straw, and even today the tea is sipped through a spoon-like little straw, often made of silver, with a tiny strainer at the end.

The systematic cultivation of Yerba maté was begun by the missionaries. They established a lively trade in the popular plant, which is called *Yeba* or Jesuit tea in Spanish. Only the leaves of young trees or shrubs were used for the trade. Between the first and second harvests the plant is allowed to rest for a year. The leaves are knocked from the stems, air-dried on open shelves or over a lively fire, and often beaten with wooden bats.

The attraction of Yerba maté tea is explained by its effect. It lends you energy when you are mentally or physically fatigued. For the Native peoples Yerba maté has the added advantage that it dampens hunger pangs. This quality has been essential to survival in times of great heat or famine.

Many tea drinkers appreciate this aspect of Yerba maté even in our own world. Since thin is considered beautiful, it is useful to know of a natural and simple way to overcome the discomfort of an empty stomach. In addition, maté is slightly laxative and diuretic.

Yerba Maté Tea

Pour boiling water over dried Yerba maté leaves, allow to sit for 5 minutes and strain. The longer you let it steep, the stronger the tea will be. It is quite all right to steep the same leaves twice. The tea can be flavored with lemon juice or maple syrup. Yerba maté tea can be purchased in the health food store, and is available in flavored versions too: lemon, Earl Grey—even chocolate!

Yerba Maté Spice Tea

Roasted Yerba maté leaves, cocoa shells, guarana seeds, coca seeds, cinnamon, allspice, star anise, a mixture of mint leaves, and cloves make a exquisite exotic tea mixture. It has to steep five minutes and can be sweetened to taste. Salus offers this tea "fermate-Krauter Gewurztee" in health food stores in North America.

Red lapacho and maté—such teas have made the healing arts of the South American Native people more appreciated by Western medicine.

Lapacho Tea—A Small Healing Miracle

In South American folk medicine, lapacho tea has its established place. It is also known as Pao D'Arco or Inca tea. It includes the wood, bark and foliage of various *Tabebuia* trees. These can live for up to seven hundred years in the higher regions of the Andes.

The bark of the lapacho tree was known to the Vikings. They exchanged the bark for precious stones and thus brought this small miracle to Europe. It is said that one of the Russian czars reached the age of one hundred and thirty because he consumed a cup of lapacho tea daily. The abbot of a Macedonian monastery, writing in AD 1305, left behind his testimony that in his day this tea was prescribed against various diseases in Europe and the Orient. The famous mountaineer Luis Trenker was said to carry a small bag of lapacho tea on all his climbs, referring to the package in his rucksack as "the treasure of the Incas."

The bark of the tree is said to have the most astonishing positive effects on human health. It is used against infections, bronchitis, asthma, stomach complaints and even cancer. The bark also acts as an anti-inflammatory. Lapacho tea is now considered one of those rare stimulants to the immune system that can improve resistance even if taken in minute doses. The substances contained in lapacho tea read like a complete "who's who" of defense champions; bio-active materials like catechins (tannins), saponin and *chinones* (for example, *lapachol*) support the immune system even in tiny quantities. Experts on lapacho believe that the tea can also impede the growth of tumors. The bark clearly does not contain a single wonder drug; the healing power of this "divine tree" is the result of its combined chemical components. If its various substances were to be used individually, the healing power would not be present.

You can drink lapacho tea at home on a regular basis, as long as you feel like it. Up to now, no negative side effects have been discovered. As with any other healing tea, however, it is a mistake to overdo it.

Make Your Own Lapacho Tea

There are two important things to remember in making this tea. First, avoid using aluminum utensils; glass, ceramic, porcelain, stainless steel or earthenware are fine. Second, do not store the tea in a plastic container or even stir it with a plastic spoon, as plastic can diminish the tea's efficacy.

For 6 cups of tea, bring that much water (1 ½ l) to a boil and add 2 slightly heaped tablespoons of lapacho tea to the water. Cover the pot, turn down the heat and let the tea simmer for 5 minutes. Remove the pot from the heat and let it steep for 15 to 20 minutes. Now strain the tea very well, preferably through cheesecloth, as even small bark fragments will eventually turn the tea bitter. Store the tea in a container, as described above. It is good cold or hot, and it is effective either way.

Lapacho Tea Mixtures

Lapacho, Killer of Colds: Prepare the tea as above, but per liter of liquid add 2 small pinches of ginger powder, a speck of cayenne and the juice of a lemon. At the first sign of a cold this tea should be drunk hot. It does the job quickly and the results are lasting. Just like elderberry, our own cold tea, lapacho cold tea will induce

sweating; and this is good, as it increases the activity of the enzymes that are going into battle against the cold germs.

Lapacho, Bringer of Desire: Prepare the tea as before. While it is brewing, add the contents of a whole vanilla bean, a heaped tablespoon of candied orange and lemon peel, and a few cloves. Just before you serve the tea to your sweetheart, place a white mound of whipped cream on top. This makes it even more pleasantly aphrodisiac.

Lapacho in the Brazilian Manner: Make the tea as usual, but instead of water use a dry white wine. Let the tea cool and add orange juice to taste. There is a story about this tea in the book *Healing with Lapacho Tea* by Walter Lübeck. Apparently, a Brazilian doctor served this tea to his brother, who was suffering from an incurable cancer. After drinking this tea daily for a month, the man is supposed to have made a complete recovery.

SanLapacho at Your Health Food Store

Health food stores sell prepared lapacho tea, often called Pao D'Arco. You can also buy the bark itself, from a herbalist or by mail order. (See the list of suppliers at the back of the book.) A relatively new tea is the SanLapacho Tea. It is augmented with potassium, calcium, iron, minerals and rosehips, which are rich in vitamin C. The tea bags are best steeped for about 5 minutes. The tea is prepared in an "ecologically correct" way, in that the trees are cultivated in large plantations and the bark is harvested in the gentlest way possible; it is peeled off with great care, so that it will replace itself and the tree can continue to grow. (See the list of suppliers at the back of the book.)

Catuaba—Pure Joy of Living

Catuaba (*Erythoxylum catuaba*) is a rain forest plant. For centuries the tea won from its bark has been highly esteemed for its ability to cheer. It calms organs and nerves and increases potency. It stimulates sexual desire and has an effect on the organs of reproduction. In Brazil they say that if a man under sixty begets a child, he did it himself, but if a man over sixty begets a child, it was catuaba! In Brazil, lapacho and catuaba are often combined. For a catuaba tea, 1 tablespoon of the bark is added to 4 cups (1 l) of boiling water, allowed to simmer for 5 minutes, set aside and allowed to steep for 15 minutes.

Angurata Tea from the Empire of the Incas

Angurata—also called heartleaf—is an age-old remedy of the Aboriginal people of Peru. Primarily, it calms an upset stomach.

Because the angurata plant (*Mentzelia cordifolia dombey*) grows in a relatively circumscribed area, its healing powers were known at first only to the people of Peru. The multitude of chemical components within the angurata plant act to impede inflammations and loosen cramps, especially in the gastrointestinal tract. Recent research has established that the plant has a strong positive impact on the immune system of the intestines, which in turn is now recognized as being a significant link in the body's overall defenses against disease. Up to now, no side effects have been found.

Preparing Your Own Angurata *Tea*
Add 1 teaspoon angurata to 1 cup (250 ml) boiling water, simmer for 7 or 8 minutes and strain. For an angurata cure, take 2 cups before

meals until your complaint has abated. Angurata stomach tea can be bought loose and in tea bags.

Special Tea Herbs of the North American Aboriginal Peoples

The Indians of North America expected each young person to acquire medical lore and to develop his or her extrasensory faculties. Ceremonies and rituals helped in this process of growth. Initiations and other celebrations often included ecstatic dances. Moreover, young men were sent off into the wilderness without food and water. As a result of fasting, they reached the limits of their endurance, went into trance states and received mystical visions. Such visions were and are taken very seriously by all the North American tribes. Although girls and women were not required to undergo this type of ordeal, great medicine women appeared quite regularly in all regions. Presumably, their innate talents and faculties brought them to the work.

Trained medicine men tended to bond in various medicine societies. Their work was supported by men who had acquired the wisdom of plants. Rituals and dances included the patient, whom these processes were meant to heal physically and simultaneously, provide with social support. At the same time, the connection to higher beings and deities was always maintained.

The shamans were a higher order of healer. While medicine men made a career choice and received the training appropriate to their trade, so to speak, shamans received a calling, manifested in the events and circumstances of their lives. Of course they had to have the basic training of the medicine man, but this was not sufficient for their work. Their therapies were more spiritual, more ecstatic, more visionary. Theirs was the realm of ceremony, cult, tradition and tribal secrets. Often they performed healing while in a trance, that is to say, in the truest sense of the word, by means of their spirit.

The concepts both of the shaman and of spiritual healing are often misused and misunderstood by people who are looking for a free ride on the First Nations bandwagon. While the European settlers almost succeeded in wiping out shamans entirely, because they regarded them as dangerous, primitive, wild men, their descendants, damaged by their own technological civilization, idealize shamans as Aboriginal saints and use them as idols in their own search for spiritual meaning.

Essiac Tea Makes an Impact

Essiac tea bears the name (spelled backwards) of the woman who became the protagonist of this mixture of herbs, Rene Caisse. The recipe came from one of the tribes that lived around the Great Lakes in Canada. The tea mix contains burdock root, sheep sorrel herb, Turkish rhubarb root and slippery elm bark, plants that strengthen the immune system and support normal functioning of the organs. The tea mixture was discovered by Rene Caisse in 1922. She found that it was the traditional remedy for cancer among some tribes in this area of Canada. Under the supervision of doctors she began using this tea with the cancer patients she visited, and achieved consistent success. Like all other conscientious herbalists, Ms. Caisse made it clear that Essiac is no panacea or miracle cure; a healthy lifestyle and stress management are

still the best way to prevent cancer. She handed her recipes to the Resperin Corporation in 1979, the year of her death.

The preparation of Essiac tea is quite complex, and all the ingredients may not be easy to find. The procedure begins by measuring out 6 ½ cups (1 ¾ l) chopped burdock root, 18 oz. (500 g) powdered sheep sorrel herb, 4 ½ oz. (125 g) powdered slippery elm bark and 1 oz. (31 g) Turkish rhubarb root. These dry ingredients must be thoroughly mixed. Any leftover herbs have to be stored in a cool, dark place to preserve their potency.

Boil water in a large pot, stir the herbs into the boiling water and simmer on a low flame for 10 minutes. Allow the covered tea to steep for 6 hours. Stir it again, then set it to steep for the same amount of time. Now heat the tea until it steams but does not boil. At this point pour it through a strainer into a second pot, then strain it a second time and put it into sterilized bottles. Store it in the refrigerator. Depending on the ailment the tea is served diluted or at full strength, once a day or several times a day. Sometimes other herbs are added too, such as dandelion root, mullein and fennel seed.

In the United States and Canada several different prepared versions of Essiac tea are available. (See list of suppliers at the end of the book.)

The Sacred Drink Utinam

Another unusual success story involves the marketing of "Original Indian Essence." This Aboriginal potion also originates in the southeast of Canada. Sales of this drink have financed a healing and training center for traditional tribal medicine. It is distributed by the Indian Wisdom Foundation, which acquired the recipe for the healing drink from an Aboriginal healer in 1995. (See list suppliers at the end of the book.) The decoction, which includes among its ingredients roots of burdock and Turkish rhubarb, sheep sorrel and slippery elm bark, as well as watercress—in other words, it is similar to Essiac—is said to free the body of wastes and to purify the spirit. According to the tribal tradition the drink called "Original Indian Essence" actually restores a person's harmony with the Great Spirit—God or the universe. Being in harmony with nature is something that the former conquerors of the New World are in dire need of these days.

EUROPE

EVERYTHING HAS EXISTED BEFORE
STORIES OF NATURAL HEALING IN EUROPE

Can we repair the sick body as we can fix a machine? Today our answer would be, not by any means. Even science, which might have replied with a resounding "yes" even twenty years ago, is now beginning to discern the complex interaction of body, mind and spirit. The concept of mechanical man is definitely outdated. Yet, back in the Roman Empire some doctors held a rather mechanical view of the body. Physicians thought that illnesses had a clear, single, immediate cause. There was no understanding at all of any larger context that might affect the individual's state of health.

Before and after that, and to this day, doctors have disagreed on matters of diagnosis and treatment. The theme is ancient, but there is one difference: before the twentieth century the mainstay of all medicine was plant power. Herbs, roots, bark, fruit and seeds of plants were made into teas, poultices and tinctures. Sometimes these helped and sometimes they did not. The world was never short of quacks.

One of the great men of medicine, whose teachings were accepted for thousands of years in Europe and elsewhere, was Galen (AD 129–99). Born Claudius Galenus in the Hellenistic city of Pergamum in western Asia Minor, he elaborated on the idea put forth by Hippocrates that there are four "humors" in the body: the four bodily fluids, blood, phlegm, black bile and yellow bile. This view of the human organism informed medical thinking in the Middle Ages, including the work of Hildegard von Bingen. Similar theories underlie Ayurvedic, Tibetan and Arab medicine.

The history of medicine has been written as a series of achievements by great men. But what of the women? What did they contribute to the history of medicine? Not much, it would seem. In fact, their contribution lay elsewhere. Women advanced medical knowledge through their works. Women of the past were not among the great theorists or scientists. They were the ones who worked in obscurity, gathering knowledge about the healing power of plants and experience in how to use them to make people better, and passing on their practical know-how to the next generation. Unfortunately, by the time the witch hunts were over, much of the knowledge that had been gathered and tended by wise women had been lost. Men took over the business of medicine. Of course, women always managed to retain some of their old love for herbs and the knowledge of how to heal with their help. Midwives continued to use herbs to facilitate birthing. In the home it was usually the women who cured the physical and mental ailments of the family with old recipes that were passed down from mother to daughter. The herbs used for these medications were collected in the immediate vicinity, in the women's own herb gardens, in the fields and under hedges. This tradition of self-medicating continued to be strong all though the nineteenth century, and many an older person still recalls fondly the homemade remedies of grandmother. Although many skeptics will deride the old ways of healing, all in all, the practitioners of phyto-therapy can stand proud before the tribunal of scientific medicine. Scientists have been busy proving so many of the claims made by herbal practitioners that it amounts to their smoothing the way for herbal medicine to re-emerge into respectability in the twenty-first century and beyond.

Hildegard von Bingen valued hops as a calming herb. The flowers of the plant are to this day included in many soporific tea recipes.

Monastic Medicine and the Herbal Healing Lore of Hildegard von Bingen

In 1998, Europeans celebrated the nine hundredth anniversary of the birth of Hildegard von Bingen. That year the books and articles about her life and work showed very clearly that medieval healing methods are still relevant to our lives. This is true first of all because Hildegard and others like her based their herbal cures on a holistic view of health, which led them to emphasize and support health maintenance and disease prevention. The second reason for the relevance of her work is that more and more people are searching for the roots of their own holistic views in the history of healing. When such people encounter monastic medicine, they are struck by the clear parallels between the medieval use of plants and contemporary natural healing methods. Today we are in a position to test the old monastic herbal remedies for their active ingredients and their uses. Our research seems to indicate that large portions of the herbal lore of the old monasteries, and especially that of Hildegard von Bingen, stand up to modern tests.

Monasteries, the Pharmacies of the Middle Ages

During the Middle Ages the prevailing knowledge of folk medicine was gathered and written down in the monasteries. As they documented this knowledge, the monasteries came to act as the pharmacies for their area of influence. Folk medicine was particularly rich in the countryside, where herb wives lived in intimate contact with nature and gathered valuable experience trying out its bounty. The old healers tended to use herbs with respect. If a recipe turned out to be reliable, it was passed on. Travelers might spread its fame. In the fourth century, hospitals started to grow up around the monasteries. They were originally hostels for those who needed a place to rest for the night (*hospis* means "guest" in Latin), but the monks also gave care and treatment to travelers who were ill or injured. The Rule of St. Benedict enjoins the monks to care for the sick as if for Christ himself. And so it is not surprising that it was monks of the Benedictine Abbey of Monte Cassino, near Naples, who first carried the seeds of southern healing plants over the Alps in order to grow them in the northern regions of Europe. The monks who worked in the hospitals were open-minded: they may have been trained in the theories of the ancient physicians, but they accepted the knowledge of folk medicine that came their way through the herbalists of the area. Thus the monks simultaneously practiced medicine according to the bodily humors of Galen and Dioscurides, and according to the practical guidelines of folk medicine.

In the twelfth century, monastic medicine reached its high point with the work of Hildegard von Bingen. This great medieval woman wrote on the subject of healing and set down many of the recipes of monastic medicine. Her thinking goes far beyond remedies, however. Her two wonderful books show an astonishing holistic vision of humankind.

Hildegard Suffered Ill Health Most of Her Life

Contemporaries described Hildegard as an impressive woman who was never healthy, all through her life. She acquired extraordinary medical knowledge, some of it through "divine showing," as she puts it in her writings. No doubt she also studied the monastic handbooks of healing, observed what happened around her and experienced the effects of healing on her own sickly body.

Hildegard was born in 1098 near Alzey, the

Sweet balm, or melissa, was first introduced to monastery gardens of northern Europe by the monks of the Benedictine order. It was called "monk's herb" and "Benedictine herb" in the Middle Ages, but its healing potential is still appreciated today by herbalists and natural healers.

tenth child of Hiltebertus von Bermersheim and his wife, Frau Mechthild. It was the time of the first Crusade, a period of great religious fervor. Hildegard started having visions at the age of three. At eight the girl was given into the loving care of Jutta von Spanheim, to live as a student in the seclusion of the small nunnery that adjoined the monastery of Disibodenberg, near Bingen. There, Hildegard took orders as a Benedictine nun, and after the death of Jutta she became the head of the convent. When she reached the age of forty-two, Hildegard received a command from God to write down her visions and make them public. Her visionary gift was confirmed by the Pope. In the year 1150 she moved to Rupertsberg, to a convent that was well equipped to alleviate physical suffering. Along with pilgrims, the sick were regularly welcomed at the gates. Behind the walls of this healing convent Hildegard produced her two books on medicine, *Physica* and *Causae et curae*.

In her book *Physica*, Hildegard describes the nature of plants, rivers, minerals and animals, and what healing powers these can manifest. Her methods derive from religious and magical healing arts. She recommends amulets and the laying on of hands. *Causae et curae* is a treatise on the cause, origin and treatment of diseases.

Despite her own chronic ill health, Hildegard undertook several preaching tours. In 1165 she founded Eibingen, a convent situated above Rüdesheim, which she henceforth visited twice each week. Now she was abbess of two convents, and she continued to conduct their business with great political acumen, even during another bout of illness that lasted three years. She was eighty-one when she died, in September 1179.

Combining Speculative and Practical Knowledge

For several reasons it is not possible to translate directly into scientific terms the medical knowledge of Hildegard von Bingen. For one thing, she used Galen's theory of the bodily humors, which is now considered outdated. Furthermore, her experience and understanding are inextricably melded with her faith and with elements of folk medicine. Nonetheless, many of her recipes are applicable today, and science can show them to work. Here is an example: The "Doctrine of Signatures" established that the appearance of a plant resembles the part of the human body that the plant can help cure. So, the heart-shaped leaf of balm (*melissa*) and its medicinal use as a tonic for the heart were obviously meant as a sign, according to Hildegard. She used melissa tea (page 120) to calm heart patients. It is a scientific fact that essential oil of melissa is an extremely effective tranquilizer for nervous conditions, migraines and all heart conditions due to nervous disorders.

The Great Healing Plants of the Medieval Monastery Garden

Most of the herbs that Hildegard von Bingen recommends through her recipes are still known in Europe. Some grow wild, while others are cultivated in herbal gardens, as formerly.

Stinging Nettle

Urtica dioca, U. urens The stinging nettle is now regarded as a weed because it has spread everywhere in response to the excessive fertilization that is ubiquitous today. Large stands of the plant are an unwelcome sight along the overly fertile edges of fields, beside brooks, in forests, by the roadside and in dumps. The plant's popularity is not boosted by the nap of stinging hair that covers the stem and the underside of the leaves. Moreover, the tips of the plant easily break off when they are touched, releasing a painful irritant that causes the skin to break out in hives.

The plant's healing power was discovered by herbalists in search of a cure for arthritic pain. In this area stinging nettle is a winner: appreciation of its extract is increasing as people realize that it is a lot cheaper than conventional medications. When it is used to complement these, it often permits a reduction in the dosage of the prescriptions, and thereby many of the side effects that anti-arthritic medications inevitably produce.

Hildegard von Bingen too relied on the healing capacity of stinging nettle. She recommends using it as a spring cleanser, to settle upset stomachs and to clear mucus congestion. She recommends using the young, ten-centimeter-high shoots of the nettle, which happen to be high in vitamin C and iron. This wild vegetable is cooked much like spinach. Another of her recipes calls for about thirty grams of these young shoots to be harvested when the moon is waxing. Puréed raw and mixed with about ⅓ cup (50 ml) olive oil, this is an effective remedy against forgetfulness and difficulty in concentrating. The mixture is applied before retiring first to the breastbone, then to the temples, and treatment continues for several months. Hildegard mentions this nettle oil in several places.

Spelt

Triticum spelta In Hildegard's nutritional plan, spelt was a basic component; she regarded it as something of a heal-all. Any therapy based on her teachings must begin with the integration of spelt into the normal diet. Nowadays, spelt products are again the fashion: they are filling the shelves of health food stores. Spelt is a grain with modest growing requirements, which has been an established staple of the European diet far longer than wheat, which was brought there from Asia. The ears of spelt are extraordinarily tough, so pests find it practically impossible to invade them. At harvest time the threshing of these hard ears requires specially built machines. Spelt used to be poor people's food, but it is now considered a valuable specialty grain. Some people like green spelt, which is harvested before the ear has ripened, but the fully ripe kernels are to be preferred due to their higher nutrient value. Spelt contains a number of vitamins, organic minerals and trace elements. While such valuable components in other grains are destroyed only during baking (which takes place at high temperatures), many of the good things in spelt are unfortunately spoilt at much lower temperatures, even in cooking.

Hildegard claimed that spelt had a cheering influence, and indeed there is a natural mood enhancer in spelt. The plant has also been shown to regulate blood pressure. The grain, furthermore, has high bioavailability, which means that starches are released into the blood throughout its digestion, unlike with wheat flour, which gives off its starches all at once. This implies that eating spelt releases less insulin, that one reaches satiety faster and that blood sugar levels do not fluctuate as much. Many people today are convinced that most gastrointestinal problems disappear when wheat is replaced in the diet by spelt.

Sweet Chestnut

Castanea sative Along with spelt, herzwein and fennel, the edible chestnut is one of the bases of the nutritional program recommended by the saintly Hildegard. Chestnuts grow in the south of Europe, mostly in Italy. In Germany, chestnut trees only thrive in the warmer wine regions. In October, when the chestnuts are ripe, they are served roasted with the young wine. This tradition is very old, going back over two thousand years. At that time both grapevines and chestnut trees were brought north by the Romans, the trees so that their wood could be used to make the stakes—Roman fashion—for the vines. Chestnuts contain vitamins A and B, phosphorus and, above all, potassium (700 mg per 100 g or 3 ½ ounces of chestnut meat). As a dietary supplement the edible chestnut is particularly helpful with heart, circulatory and kidney disorders. Hildegard recommends eating chestnuts against all forms of weakness and in order to maintain good health. In the Middle Ages chestnut trees

grew everywhere near vineyards, and they held a fascination for Hildegard because of the enormous, almost magical healing powers ascribed to them. She recommends the leaves, bark and seeds against gout, headaches and chest pains, as well as depression, something we no longer agree with. Today, however, the leaves of the chestnut contribute to drugs against bronchitis and whooping cough. The tannin-rich seeds of the chestnut are also supposed to be helpful against diarrhea.

Marshmallow

Althea officinalis Marshmallow is a very powerful plant that was used in Greek and Roman times against coughs. It eventually found its way over the walls of the monastic gardens and into the gardens of the farmers' wives. In Germany a lot of marshmallow is found in the surroundings of the former convents and monasteries, and the area where Hildegard had her nunneries is no exception. The plant grows as high as 5 feet (1 ½ m); the leaves are thickly matted with fine hair. The flower petals are reddish-white and surrounded by a calyx. In monastic medicine the fresh herb was used. Hildegard recommends it against a chesty cough, and her advice is supported by our own doctors. In contrast to the teachings of the medical tradition of her day, she also used a drink of marshmallow against fevers and, in the form of compresses, against headaches. In our own lives the mallow family is represented by the edible fruit of one member (*Hibiscus esculentus*), which is known as okra or gumbo. It is an important part of the cuisine of the southern United States.

Andorn was recommended by Hildegard for sore throat.

considered capable of miraculous cures by herbalists in the Middle Ages. Hildegard too recommends them, against lung and liver diseases. Contemporary naturopaths use the plant in cases of cranial trauma, concussion and headache. It is possible to buy a powder made of the dried leaves.

Spogel Seed

Plantago ovata Of this plantain, a southern ribwort related also to psyllium, Hildegard used mostly the seeds. Because of the seeds' ability to swell up, which is even greater than that of flax seeds, it is useful in treating constipation and slow peristalsis. Spogel seeds do have to swell up completely before use, however, and when they are taken, it is imperative to drink lots of water or tea. For each tablespoon of plantain one should drink 1 cup (250 ml) of liquids. For a slight stimulation of the intestines it is possible to strew spogel seeds over your spelt soup or yogurt. The seeds can absorb ten times their weight in water.

Hart's Tongue Fern

Phyllitis scolopendrium The hart's tongue fern loves alkaline soil; it prefers to grow on shady walls of rocky, moist ravines, and on high trees. The plant is rare except in Alpine regions of Europe. It is not native to the Americas. Hart's tongue fern produces slightly wavy leaves between 6 and 20 inches (15–50 cm) long, arranged in a rosette. The long, undivided leaves are reminiscent of a tongue. These leaves were

Wild Thyme

Thymus serpyllum It was known in the Middle Ages as a magic herb and a folk remedy. Hildegard called the plant "field thyme." She used it fresh, finely crushed or as a dry powder. Like the related Mediterranean thyme, wild thyme is cooked with food. Among healing plants it figures as a cure for rash, neurodermatitis and eczema.

Quince

Cydonia oblonga The quince is a plant of the rose family. The tree or shrub can attain up to 20 feet (6 m) in height. Although the quince tree stems from the Caucasus mountain range, its name refers back to the city of Kydonia on the island of Crete. (The Latin for quince was *cydonia mala*, "apples from Cydonia.") It is assumed that the sacred fruit of Venus was actually the quince. Hildegard recommends the cooked or baked fruit against gout and "augmented saliva flow." She also claims that quinces can be eaten raw when they are completely ripe. Natural healers of today recommend eating quince sauce cooked with the skins and puréed, for arthritis. With rash, eczema and swellings, the seeds are supposed to help, cooked to a jelly in water and applied externally.

Greater Celandine

Chelidonium majus Take your kids on a walk past a dump and they will run for the fine yellow flowers of the greater celandine, which thrive in that setting in large colonies. Before they pluck the flowers, however, you must sternly call them back and warn them, just as Hildegard warned us. The slimy juice of the celandine is poisonous and may not be eaten. It is also sticky, so that it comes off your hands only after much scrubbing and the use of creams. The greater celandine is related to the opium poppy, and it has its own powers for calming the nerves, alleviating pain and loosening cramps. The flower, which has four petals, turns into a podlike capsule with four seeds. Hildegard recommended the greater celandine against warts and swellings. For this purpose, only chopped roots and leaves are used, soaked overnight in vinegar. The plant mush is then applied (only externally!) to warts and welts and covered with bandages.

Greater Plantain

Plantago major, P. media, P. lanceolata In many European families it is still common knowledge that when your skin gets stung by the nettle, you simply rub the sore spot with a crushed leaf of the greater plantain. It is also eased by the fresh juice of the greater plantain and the smaller, hoary plantain. She also used the plant as a disinfectant, and a tea brewed from the leaves served her in treating colds. All around the globe it is primarily the broad plantain, with its wide, rounded leaves, that is found in meadows and around fields. One interesting use of the greater plantain by Hildegard was against the acute pain in the side of the body caused by running, called "the stitch"; the leaves are laid on the stitch after being parboiled and squeezed in a towel. Against gout the juice of the leaves is strained through a cloth, mixed with wine and honey, and administered three times a day in a liqueur glass.

Wormwood

Artemisia absinthium This bitter herb is one of the most significant healing plants in Hildegard's pharmacy. Typical of the family of *compositae*, wormwood has an intricately divided leaf and loose-branching flower heads. Hildegard thought the plant might be the "master against all exhaustion." As a salve she used it against colds and gout. Contemporary medicine appreciates wormwood for its bitter qualities, which have an acknowledged record in fighting disturbances of the digestion, gallbladder and liver. It is therefore likely that the following remedy for melancholy would work; it is known today that depression is a common symptom accompanying liver problems. Here is Hildegard's prescription: "Wormwood, if it is fresh, should be crushed and its juice squeezed out through a cloth. It should be added to boiled wine and honey so that the taste of the juice is more prominent than that of the wine and honey." Hildegard recommends a liqueur glass of this drink to be taken on an empty stomach every third day from May to October. This therapy is supposed to strengthen the heart and lungs, cleanse the gut and improve digestion. And this drink is not to be mistaken for inexpensive vermouth!

THE PRECIOUS HEALING POTIONS OF SAINT HILDEGARD VON BINGEN

In Hildegard's time it was not customary to make teas based on water. Herbs, roots and seeds were usually simmered in wine, soaked in wine or made into powders that could be mixed with wine. From the point of view of contemporary herbal therapy, the combination of herbs with wine still makes good sense. The two substances can enhance each other's virtues. On the one hand, the alcohol in wine can dissolve not just the water-soluble but the fat-soluble chemicals in the plants; on the other hand, it is more efficient than water in carrying the substances into the blood. Moderation is recommended with these tasty herbal libations, however. Hildegard spaces her potions over the course of the day, served always in small liqueur glasses.

Warning: If for any reason you cannot drink alcohol, please confine yourself to the water-based tea recipes.

Stinging Nettle for Arthritic Pain

Whereas Hildegard recommends this tea against worms, modern herbal healers consider it useful against rheumatic complaints. To prepare the tea as it is given here you will need a juicer. If this recipe is too troublesome for you, you may find a similar prepared mixture in your health food store.

1 part stinging nettle juice
*1 part cotton grass (*Eriophorum*) juice*
Walnut tree leaves, amounting to the same weight as the two juices combined
1 squirt vinegar
Much honey
About 6 cups (1 ½ l) water

Preparation and use: Bring all ingredients, except for the honey, to a boil, skim off the foam and strain out the plant debris. Sweeten with honey before drinking. With respect to the dosage, Hildegard says: "For 15 days you should drink this in moderate amounts on an empty stomach, but after meals, abundantly." If you opt for the packaged tea, take 2 cups a day for 2 weeks.

Cough Potion with Lovage

Lovage was an important plant in the medieval monastery garden. Hildegard used it for coughs and against lung and chest complaints.

0.2 oz. (5 g) lovage
0.2 oz. (5 g) sage
0.7 oz. (20 g) fennel
2 cups (500 ml) wine

Preparation and use: Place the herbs in the wine and let them steep for 1 or 2 days, until the wine has absorbed their taste. Strain the wine and heat a small glassful to drink after meals. Hildegard writes that if your cough is mild, you need not heat the wine.

Heart and Nerve Tea with Melissa to Raise the Spirits

Sweet or lemon balm was cultivated mostly by monks in the Middle Ages, and so it came to be called monk's or priest's herb. The characteristic aroma and taste of this popular plant are

Hildegard's medical teachings give instructions for turning healing plants, like eucalyptus, mallow and cotton grass, into alcoholic tinctures and herbal wines.

pleasant and lemony. Contemporary phytotherapy counts balm among the classic carminatives, in that it relieves dyspepsia due to nervous disorders and anxiety. It has a cheering effect all of its own, as the saintly Hildegard well knew. This drink warms and lightens the heart. The potion's effect on the heart is derived from the medieval doctrine of "signatures," which teaches that a leaf's shape is the signature of the human organ that the plant can heal. Because of its leaflike shape, melissa must relate to the heart, and indeed balm was also known as "heart herb."

1 tbsp. fresh leaves of sweet balm
2 cups (500 ml) water

Preparation and use: Bring the melissa leaves to a boil in the water, remove from the heat and allow to steep. Drink several cups of this, spread out over the day.

Monastic Melissa Spirits

Spirit of melissa is an ancient alcoholic heal-all, used to treat every kind of ailment, and it is experiencing a renaissance today. Whether it is headaches, nervous tension or insomnia, internal or external, all problems of life are relieved by the delectable Carmelite's Spirits, as this melissa wine was called. You can make it yourself.

7 oz. (200 g) fresh melissa leaves
4 cups (1 l) 60-proof brandy

Preparation and use: Add the fresh balm leaves to the brandy, seal the container well and let sit for about 10 days. Strain the herbs through a cotton cloth and wring out the liquid. Dosage: no more than 10 to 20 drops a day. You can take your spirit of balm in a cup of hot water or balm tea, but don't drink more than 2 cups a day.
Warning: This medicine is not suitable for children.

Tea for Colds

The dog, or wild, rose has been esteemed as a valuable healing herb since the Middle Ages. The plant's pink blossoms are recommended in Hildegard's book as much as its red hips, which we prize for their extraordinarily high content of vitamin C. This would be the rationale for prescribing rosehip tea for a cold. Rosehips can be harvested fresh from the shrub until late fall, and they can be used together with the leaves.

1 tsp. dried or chopped rosehips
1 cup (250 ml) water

Preparation and use: Chop the fruit fine and cover with 1 cup of boiling water. Let the tea steep for 10 minutes. Drink it hot when a cold is just beginning. At the same time, while the cold is still building in strength, it is a good idea to take some echinacea to give the immune system a boost.

Tea for Bloating

The classic anti-bloat tea to give to colicky babies is made of fennel, anise and caraway. It is also suitable for lactating mothers, as the effects of the tea are passed on to the baby through the milk. It is possible to buy this tea in the health food store, but you can prepare it yourself.

Remember: the anise and fennel seeds have to be crushed in a mortar to release their active components.

Equal parts of:
Fennel seeds
Anise fruit
Caraway seeds

Preparation and use: 1 teaspoon of this mixture is brewed with 1 cup (250 ml) boiling water. Cover the cup and let the tea steep for about 10 minutes. Strain before drinking. You and your baby can have as much of this tea as you wish.

Oat Straw Tea

"He feels his oats" is an expression that is sometimes applied to a lively, energetic young person. Oats are considered an energy food and, as such, prime fare for children and the ailing. The grain contains biologically valuable forms of protein and fat. Oat starch is so easy to digest that it begins breaking down while it is still being chewed. Green oats, harvested just before they bloom, deliver the most important active ingredients in their juice. The tea made of the "still green" grain was an ancient folk remedy in Hildegard's time and is still used today. Nowadays it is employed to free the body of harmful waste products. It is particularly useful in cases of arthritic joint inflammation and when the uric acid level in the urine is high, as in cases of gout. Green straw tea will release harmful metabolic by-products and simultaneously remove unnecessary water held in the tissues. Naturally, you may be able to obtain the ingredients for this tea fresh, but if not, your health food store offers dried oat straw and ready-made teas. In these, the role of the other herbs is to support the action of the oat straw.

2.7 oz. (75 g) oat straw
0.4 oz. (10 g) stinging nettle
0.2 oz. (5 g) alpine lady's mantle (Alchemilla alpina)
0.4 oz. (10 g) St. John's wort

Preparation and use: First mix all of these dry ingredients well; this is your tea blend. Now add 1 to 2 tablespoons of the mixture to 2 or 3 cups (500–750 ml) of boiling water. Simmer the herbs for about 20 minutes. An alternative method is to start the tea cold, letting the herbs steep for several hours. The tea only needs 10 minutes of simmering and 10 minutes of steeping before it is ready to strain. The dosage: 3 cups daily, if possible, unsweetened.

Spogel Seed Wine

In connection with this tea the saintly Hildegard spoke of "fever of the stomach," against which she claimed it will help. In today's parlance one could perhaps speak of an upset or inflamed stomach. Try it out:

1–2 tsp. spogel seeds
1 cup (250 ml) wine
or
a handful of spogel seed herb (Plantago ovata) *or ispaghul*
2 cups (500 ml) wine

Preparation and use: Bring the wine and the seeds or herb to a boil and strain the decoction.

Drink it warm. An additional relaxing benefit is supplied by the external application of the boiled seeds or herb in the form of a compress. Just fold them in a cloth and apply warm to the area of the cramped stomach.

Headache Tea of Juniper Berries

This old home remedy has been found to help most with headaches that have no physical cause.

0.1 oz. (3 g) juniper berries
1 cup (250 ml) water

Preparation and use: Crush the juniper berries and pour boiling water over them. Let them steep for 5 minutes and strain. You can drink 3 cups of freshly brewed tea per day.

Blueberry Tea for the Bladder

This tea is helpful for a weak bladder, for example after a bladder infection. It is said to help with hemorrhoids too.

Fresh or dried blueberry leaves
1 cup (250 ml) water

Preparation and use: Chop the fresh or dried leaves and use about 1 teaspoon per cup of water. Pour the boiling water over the leaves and allow to steep for about 10 minutes. Drink several cups of this tea per day, as needed.

Energy Tea

When the January blahs are weighing down your spirits, when you feel sluggish and without pep, when you don't feel like doing anything any more—this tea will get you going again.

2 tsp. powdered anise root
1 cup (250 ml) water

Preparation and use: Mix the powder with cold water, bring to a short boil and strain. You can drink this amount spread throughout the day, in small sips.

Bitter Tea for the "Bitter Day"

It seems that bitter substances have been largely eliminated from our daily diet. This is unfortunate, because bitters stimulate alkalinity and

Devil's claw, mallow and lavender remain to this day the favorite plants of phyto-medicine.

counteract the widespread problem of hyper-acidity within the entire metabolism. "Base-generators," like the bitter tea that follows, are a comfort and a blessing. For one thing they slim the body as they de-acidify it. It is a good idea to designate one day a week as "bitter day," when you drink this tea several times. It is also good to eat basic foods that day, such as salads and steamed bitter vegetables. These include artichoke, watercress, chicory, endive, nasturtium, dandelion leaves, arugula and ribwort. This is a way to induce your body to rid itself of its acidic wastes. Bitter herbs also do a job on the mental plane, making it easier to purge old patterns of thought and obsolete concepts.

Angelica root
Root of gentian
Dandelion
Centaury (erythraea)
Wormwood
Fennel
Melissa
Sage
3 cups (750 ml) water

Preparation and use: Make a dry mixture of equal parts angelica, gentian, dandelion, centaury and wormwood. This will constitute at least 70 percent of the total tea mixture. The other 30 percent is made of equal parts fennel, melissa and sage. Mix this tea blend well. Pour 1 cup (250 ml) boiling water over 1 teaspoon of the tea, cover and allow to stand for about 10 minutes. Drink this tea unsweetened against all disorders of the digestive process, especially those that are due to over-acidity.

Note to this recipe: "Bitter is better" is a saying of Ayurvedic medicine. This refers not only to the taste but to a certain energetic quality of bitter foods that has almost completely disappeared from the essential victuals we consume today. Ayurvedic medicine teaches that foods with a bitter taste have the power to correct ailments caused by twisted or churning energy. This is the reason why many medicines taste bitter.

The Story of Witches and Wise Women

What real witches used to do is done today by a variety of alternative health practitioners. Many witches were powerful, courageous, authentic and knowledgeable women who relied on and acted from their intuition. They were healers, magicians and individualists. They were most familiar with nature and plant spirits, and herbs constituted their chief source of healing, magic and food. Herbs were brewed into healing elixirs. Herbs also formed the basis of the magic potions used in their rituals.

In pre-Christian times, the women that were later called witches were the pagan priestesses. Their advice was sought in all of life's quandaries. They were held in awe, but they were also feared because they maintained very special connections to the higher powers. They could foretell the future and ask the gods for their advice, but they also had the courage to look the devil in the eye. They understood magic, white or black, as the case might be. These women did things that ordinary mortals did not dare attempt.

For example, they undertook soul journeys. It seems that it was mostly the "wild women" who were willing to cross the symbolic line that separates the here and now from what is beyond. The magic herbs that the witches used to take them on their "trips" were indeed hallucinogenic, as, for instance, henbane, which was also called *Belinuntia*. The syllable *bhel* means "fancy"—and the fancy is certainly stimulated in a very powerful way by henbane, which was an initiatory drug of black magicians. Given the right dose, it will propel the soul on a journey, but it will be a trip into an unpredictable realm of darkness. The contemporary healer and witch Margaret Madejski writes about these soul journeys as follows: "The initiation, which they underwent through the use of these mind-expanding herbs, involved near-death experiences. Visions of tunnels, nature spirits, death and the devil combines with feelings of flying, floating and falling. Those drug-induced dreams granted the original witches glimpses into the realms of the Gods and of spirits." It was rumored that just chewing a leaf or two of henbane would bring on hallucinations of horned denizens of hell. The flowers of the henbane, with their nauseous, moldy smell and purplish black veins, are not called "devil's eyes" for nothing.

Whereas such an excursion into the other world is by no means safe for most of us (henbane can cause drug psychoses), the witches of old knew how to deal with the mighty plant spirits. They also used henbane to heal, for in small doses the magic herb serves to relax the mind, loosen cramped muscles and ease pain.

As with henbane, the herb women employed other herbs for many diverse purposes. The same plant might be used for contraception, to cause an abortion and in a love potion. Herbs accompanied wise women into all situations of life. They would gird their loins with herbal weapons, taking courage and strength from them. Armed with the fragrance of herbal incense and the power of ritual, they accompanied people into death, saved lives and stood by birthing mothers during their hours of labor. And when their work as midwives was done, they lovingly prepared the traditional herbal childbed to heal the new mother. (See page 137.)

And then the time of the witch hunts arrived. The result was that the wisdom accumulated over centuries by these practitioners of folk medicine was forgotten. As the witches were bedeviled, the herbs they had used were devalued in two different ways: either they were dismissed as

useless or they were said to be dangerous and deadly poisonous. And so it happened that for many centuries scores of healing plants were not used in Europe at all. A relative of the American yam, for example, that grows in Europe was honored as a desirable contraceptive in the time of the "good witches." It is referred to as "pain root," and after the witch hunts it was literally "withdrawn from the market." It was not until the beginning of the twentieth century that the plant was rediscovered. Today, the pill is still made in part from active ingredients contained in this species of the lily family.

Much like the plants of the wise women, the women themselves were reassessed, and they were categorized in one of two ways: they were either good mothers or bad witches. Witches were impugned for turning themselves and others into wild beasts in order to be safe from attack. Harmful magic was now said to be the stock-in-trade of witches: they would poison man and beast or plant poisonous herbs throughout the fields to spoil the whole harvest. Another common fantasy was that by means of their witch's balm or flying unguent, witches could move through the air. This much was of course true—during their soul journeys. Nor were suspicions of orgies among the "wild women" completely unjustified. Using herbal potions to release their inhibitions, they were said to dance ecstatically at the Witches' Sabbath, and they were suspected of "consorting with the devil."

Even though many contemporary women are turning to the old lore of the wise women and want to try out the power of herbs, it is necessary to issue a warning against the mighty plant spirits. Experimenting alone with the hallucinogenic plants of the nightshade family is strictly contraindicated. The reasons are well stated by Hans Peter Dürr: "The deadly nightshades make us hot as a tomcat, blind as a bat, dry as a bone, red as a beet, and crazy as a hen."

Mysterious Magic Plants from the Witches' Tradition

Witches' herbs are classified into four groups according to their use:

- poisonous plants for harmful magic
- plants that deliver drugs for the soul's flight
- women's plants, used for contraception, birth and abortion
- herbs used as sexual stimulants

Of course the classification of any one plant is seldom cut and dried; but knowing the subtleties of that sort of thing is exactly what witchcraft is about. Furthermore, a good deal of experience is needed to find the right dose for each situation, especially where the hallucinogens are concerned. Since mandrake, henbane and other poisonous plants are counted among the witches' herbs, they are here described for the sake of completeness; this does not mean that they are meant to be used.

Poisonous, Hallucinogenic Plants

Mandrake

Mandragora officinarum Mandrake is the classic magic herb of the Middle Ages. The plant still grows in certain parts of southern Europe, for example Greece and Cyprus. The plant's root does indeed resemble a man, with its habit of forking into two leg like parts, and shooting out on the sides into "arms." In ancient Greece boiled mandrake was a household remedy for swellings. Later in history it served various purposes: to induce vomiting, as an anesthetic during surgery, as an abortive suppository and to induce sleep.

Many strange beliefs and stories clung to this witch's herb, which it has not been able to shake off to this day. It is said that mandrake root may be dug up only during the night, and only when the moon is full. A black dog, symbolizing the hound of hell, has to be present; only thus can the digger survive the dreadful shrieks of the mandrake as it is dragged from the soil. One is also advised to make an offering to the spirit of the plant before setting out on the hazardous task of digging it up. A circle is drawn around the plant and wine is poured into it as an offering, or one can offer silver instead. It is said that people who follow these precautions will find that henceforth the plant's spirit protects their house faithfully. If you disregard these safety measures, however, it will go ill with you for a long time after you dig up the mandrake—if you do not drop dead when you hear it shriek!

Henbane

Hyoscyamus niger After the mandrake root, henbane was the most important trance-inducing plant used by the witches of old. The annual form of henbane grows all over Europe, even along roads. The flower has been described as "dingy yellow . . . marked with a close network of lurid purple veins." The plant, which exhibits a great range of variation in appearance and habit, is said to be poisonous in all its parts. It was also used by the Druids. The Celts are said to have brought it into play when they wanted to prophesy or to induce visions or waking dreams. It also served in the rituals in honor of the god Bil, whose name probably contributed to the German name for the herb, *Bilsenkraut*.

Impressions of the witch's kitchen: burdock, roots, ivy and hemp seeds.

Many different cultures have used henbane to ease pain. It is equally useful in love potions, to make women more cooperative. Some members of Wicca, the contemporary religious cult of witches, still use henbane. It is an ingredient in an oil that is rubbed into the area of the third eye to encourage vision.

Yew

Taxus All parts of this tree seem to be poisonous. The yew has been a sacred tree for longer than we can remember. The Druids used to assemble under yews, and the witches took over this tradition. The yew is the quintessential witch's tree. They carve their broomsticks out of yew wood. If you wish to experience the secret of the yew, sit under one on a hot day or a warm, humid night. Under such weather conditions the yew will give off a volatile, psychoactive substance called *taxine*. After ten minutes you will feel intoxicated, and it might even be that you will see nature spirits. They say in Germany that sitting under the yew tree is like putting your head in granny's lap.

Hemlock

Conium maculatum This umbelliferous, poisonous plant is mentioned in all books on witchcraft. Both the water hemlock (cowbane) and the spotted hemlock were classic analgesics and anesthetics in the early history of medicine. The high induced by hemlock gave witches the feeling that they had changed into animals. This is because the active ingredients in hemlock change the skin's tactile perception, making it possible to think that one is covered with, say, the fur of a cat or the feathers of an owl.

Hemp

Cannabis sativa Today, hemp is considered a dangerous drug, its effects are the subject of scientific controversies and its use is a legal conundrum. For the original witches it was simply an important ingredient in many of their recipes. It was esteemed not only for the mind-expanding states it induces, but because it eases pain. It was also said that cannabis serves the dance of love. The witches of old are reported to have found and exploited another gift of hemp: they used it to alter their perceptions to the point where they were capable of seeing the spirits of plants.

Deadly Nightshade or Devil's Cherries

Atropa belladonna The deadly nightshade is an imposing, even conspicuous, shrub with large leaves and shiny black berries. A native of the warm south, belladonna is now grown anywhere in Europe and is considered to be the most poisonous plant in the region. Eating even a few berries, which are said to be very sweet, can cause death. The name belladonna, meaning "beautiful woman," originated in the time of the witch trials. During the Renaissance many beautiful ladies used deadly nightshade as a cosmetic for the skin.

Modern medicine uses the plant as well. Ophthalmologists add a drop of belladonna to the eye to dilate the pupil and reveal the back of the eyeball. Homeopathy also considers the plant to be of great importance.

Non-poisonous Witches' Plants

Those herbs that are not poisonous were used by the wise women in treating women's health issues, from premenstrual syndrome, through

fertility problems and childbirth, to menopause. Nowadays, midwives with a knowledge of plants and gynecologists with a bent for natural healing are rediscovering this ancient female lore.

Lady's Mantle

Alchemilla vulgaris It is said that the neatly toothed edge of the leaf, which was associated with the mantle of the Virgin, gave this small plant its name. Like many other plants whose names contain a reference to a woman or mother, lady's mantle is primarily suitable for the treatment of female complaints. It will relieve the pains that come with menstruation, reduce excessive bleeding, and help with discharges and inflammations of the vagina. Because of its astringent quality and high tannin content, *Alchemilla* is also useful in treating injuries and external inflammations. Lady's mantle tea is an old remedy for gastrointestinal upsets, diarrhea and gastritis, whereas for the management of women's disorders the tincture is preferred nowadays.

Warning: Lady's mantle stimulates the uterus and should not be taken by pregnant women.

Mugwort

Artemisia vulgaris Mugwort or St. John's plant grows by the wayside today, as it did in ancient Greece. It was there that it was first named after Artemis, the goddess of the hunt. Greek physicians used mugwort as a women's herb, and especially as a birth-promoting plant. Mugwort increases the blood flow to the uterus and thereby acts as a mild aphrodisiac, promotes conception and regulates the menses. Formerly, mugwort was an important component of the herbal childbed the midwife prepared to heal the mother after delivery; it also included lady's mantle, rue, thyme and monk's pepper (*agnus castus*). All the herbs that the midwives collected for the mother's protection have since been shown to have antibiotic components.

Warning: The use of mugwort should be avoided during pregnancy and lactation. Since the herb stimulates the uterus, its use can lead to malformations of the fetus. And during breast-feeding, the active ingredient *thujon* can be transmitted to the baby through the mother's milk.

Vervain

Verbena officinalis Vervain is native to Europe, where it will grow in stony places, in empty lots and by the roadside. It is a typical women's herb. Midwives used it for "birth magic." To this day midwives who know their herbs use tea of vervain to speed the birth. The active ingredient *verbenaline* induces labor. Witches counted it among the "belt herbs," displaying magic related to love and fertility. At midsummer night the thing to wear was a belt plaited of vervain.

Warning: Do not use vervain during pregnancy. It can bring on labor prematurely and cause a miscarriage.

Tea Recipes Using the Herbs of the Wise Women

All the recipes here are—without exception—non-poisonous, harmless and free of black magic. The herbs come from the "white" section of the witch's kitchen. We are using the same healing plants that women have employed since time immemorial to manage their own affairs, including the hard parts. In fact, the teas in this section are really suitable only for women.

Menopause Tea

This tea is a great companion through the stages of menopause. At a time when everything you have been used to becomes questionable, when body and soul are in an uproar, when hormones go wild, it is a real comfort to sip a tea like this. The herbs in it release ingredients that resemble hormones and gently regulate the body, thereby calming the spirit. Margaret Madejski, a herbal practitioner who lives in Munich, Germany, has been prescribing this tea for many years to all her menopausal patients, almost as a standard mixture. She has discovered that most women find it so soothing that they require no other medication to handle their difficulties. One of the many benefits of this tea, for example, is that it normalizes perspiration. At the onset of menopause one or two cups a day will be quite sufficient. When the sweat is running down your face, it is time to drink the tea regularly.

Lady's mantle
Hop cones
Sage leaves
Melissa leaves
Walnut leaves
2 cups (500 ml) water

Preparation and use: The above ingredients should be thoroughly mixed and then stored. To make the tea, take 2 to 3 tablespoons of the tea mixture, pour 2 cups (500 ml) water over them and allow to steep for 3 to 5 minutes. Sweetening the brew with honey helps the body absorb the active ingredients. The best way to use this tea is over a 6- to 8-week period, with 2 cups (500 ml) of the tea being consumed over the course of each day. The tea therapy should then be stopped for at least 1 week. It can be resumed if needed.

Note to this Recipe: The three main ingredients of menopause tea—lady's mantle, hops and walnut leaves—have served for thousands of years in the treatment of women's disorders. Lady's mantle used to be the base of most such female recipes. The small green plant was once sacred to Freya, the Germanic goddess of love and fertility. During the menopausal years the herb serves women in a different way, namely, by regulating sweating. This effect of lady's mantle was explained by wise women—who tended to observe their plants very closely—by the fact that the plant itself "sweats." Around ten in the morning the leaves are covered with drops of liquid extruded by the pores, just like drops of sweat. Sage leaves lessen perspiration too, while the cones of hops are chosen for their estrogenlike active ingredient. These chemicals are able to alleviate the side effects of the body's diminished estrogen levels. With the help of this tea it is therefore possible that some women, who are suspicious of synthetic estrogen therapy, can avoid this procedure entirely.

*A **suggested combination:*** Another phyto-hormonal menopause aid is pomegranate seeds.

Many cultures have considered the pomegranate a symbol of fertility and rejuvenation. The plentiful seeds of the fruit are a clear indication that it will increase fertility, and therefore desire. And the seeds do indeed contain a natural estrogen, which is close in composition to that formed in the human ovaries. Our tip is to augment the menopausal tea therapy by eating some pomegranate seeds every day. They should be as fresh as possible; chew them well and swallow them.

Warning: Pomegranate seeds may not be taken during pregnancy or during any illness that precludes the use of estrogen. If you are planning a longer pomegranate cure, you should definitely consult your physician or health practitioner.

Moon Flow Tea

Many women who have trouble with their monthly cycle can improve their plight by co-ordinating their monthly flow with the rhythm of the moon. Optimally, ovulation occurs on the full moon and menstruation on the new moon. This Moon Flow Tea can help to harmonize the two monthly cycles. The tea is recommended for women whose periods are weak, irregular or intermittent, or whose cycle is simply too long. All of these symptoms mean that the female organism is not able to shed all the toxins that the regular monthly flow is meant to eliminate from the body. Typical symptoms of irregular and weak menses are depressive episodes and an imperfect complexion. These things often result when the self-cleaning mechanisms of the body have slowed or stopped functioning. In such situations it is a good thing to have mugwort on hand to restore order.

3 tbsp. dried or fresh mugwort leaves
2 cups (500 ml) water

Preparation and use: Pour 2 cups (500 ml) water over the mugwort leaves and allow them to steep for about 10 minutes. Pour the tea into your Thermos bottle and drink it warm over the course of the whole day.

Important: In order to encourage a weak flow it is best to begin the mugwort therapy at least a week before your next period. If your menses frequently fail to manifest, even though you are not pregnant, you would do well to drink this tea for two weeks as the moon wanes. After two or three months menstruation will resume, and it will begin as planned—on the new moon.

Note to this recipe: Mugwort has been a lunar herb since before history began. The plant's Latin name, *Artemisia vulgaris*, shows this, for Artemis was a moon goddess. In the witches' kitchen, however, mugwort had other functions than aligning women's lives to the moon. The herb served as a general detoxifying remedy and as a spice in fatty dishes. This latter use of the herb derives from its ability to stimulate the digestion. Since the plant increases blood flow to the entire lower abdominal area, it was also valued as a fertility booster and mild aphrodisiac.

For general detoxification: Women who do not suffer from problems with their cycle can still avail themselves of the cleansing powers of mugwort. After all, this herb can lighten depressed spirits as it goes about its work of cleaning out the body. The tea for this purpose is prepared as follows:

3 tbsp. mugwort leaves
Honey
2 cups (500 ml) water

Preparation and use: Add the herb to the cold water with some honey and bring it all to a short boil. Drink this daily dose in small amounts over the course of the day.

Warning: This mugwort recipe, no less than the other, should be taken only when the moon is waning, that is, between full moon and new moon. It is important to drink it only as long as your sweat still has an odor. Once the odor stops, you know that the cleansing is complete.

Dream Oracle Tea

This is a genuine witches' recipe, offering magic for women who like to dive into the world of dreams and trances in search of answers to life's questions. It is even rumored that many a woman looking for a partner has seen him in a dream after drinking this tea. Actually, Dream Oracle Tea will help any woman who desires an enhanced connection with her inner or intuitive self or is facing a major decision. The recipe intensifies the intuition and tends to deliver answers in dreams or daydreams. During this time it is a good idea to pay close attention to hunches and visions.

3 handfuls forget-me-not flowers, picked by you

Preparation and use: The seeker should collect about 3 handfuls of forget-me-not flowers without stems in a beautiful place. Inside the house, the flowers are spread on a sheet of paper on the windowsill. The moon should shine on the blossoms for at least 3 nights.

Each night after that, remove as many blossoms as you can grasp between two fingers and thumb, place them in a cup, add boiling water and cover the cup. Let your blossoms steep for 10 minutes.

Warning: Before you drink your Dream Oracle Tea, formulate your question and contemplate it intensively, taking it inside. You can think of your question as you go to bed and fall asleep. If the goddess of fate wishes to help you, the answer—it is said—will appear in a dream. So that you do not forget your dream, write it down immediately upon waking. Make sure that you place paper and pen beside your bed before you retire.

Note to this recipe: The wise herbwives knew that forget-me-not blossoms have a direct connection to the element of air, to the sky, and therefore to the realm of inspiration. The sky blue and sunshine yellow of the flowers symbolize the colors of the firmament. They show that, through them, advice can come from above. The moon, which shines upon the flowers, is only the means by which the answers enter the flowers, but the advice really manifests in the dream, a daydream or a trance state.

Tea for Love and Fertility Magic

The mysterious secret of aphrodisiac potions has been revealed to science: herbs with estrogenlike ingredients stimulate blood flow into the organs of the lower abdomen. Thus they are not merely sexually exciting, but they also increase fertility. Women who often suffer from menstrual cramps will also enjoy the relaxing and cramp-loosening effects of the herbs in this tea.

Rue
Vervain
Mugwort leaves
Damiana leaves
2 cups (500 ml) water

Preparation and use: To prepare your tea blend, mix 2 parts rue and 1 part each of the other 3 herbs. Cover 3 tablespoons of the tea mixture with 2 cups (500 ml) boiling water. After steeping for 10 minutes, the strained tea can be drunk any time over the course of the day, up to a maximum of 3 cups a day. If menstrual cramps are the bane of your life, drink this tea for a week before your period is supposed to begin.

Note to this recipe: Rue is one of the oldest of the witches' herbs. The wise women of the Middle Ages used it to cure just about any female complaint. Rue was even drawn on to attempt abortions, which is why in Germany it used to be called "herb of the beautiful girls." In the prudish eighteenth century the use of rue was forbidden to women because it was likely to evoke unchaste thoughts. In old herb gardens in the European countryside you may still find rue being tended with other plants, though this is now more likely to happen south of the Alps. It also grows wild in warmer regions.

Extra tip: Whenever you want to have a strong libido, you can bathe in this Love and Fertility Magic. Brew a handful of the blend in 7 cups

(2 l) of water and strain after 10 minutes. Then add this tea to your bathwater.

Tea to Strengthen the Erotic Aura

This is not a joke: there are teas that will alter the body odor of a woman in such a way that men will notice her more. The scents of certain "love blossoms" are used here to boost feminine attractiveness.

1 handful cherry blossoms
1 handful rose blossoms (it must be
Rosa centifolia)
1 handful linden blossoms, whole or rubbed
2 cups (500 ml) water

Preparation and use: At the time of the full moon in April, at about 10 in the morning, collect your handful of cherry blossoms from a tree and spread them flat to dry. Mix them, when dry, with equal amounts of rose and linden blossoms. Take 1 tablespoon of the mixture, cover it with the boiling water, let stand, covered, for 10 minutes and then strain. Take your aphrodisiac potion with a tablespoon of honey about an hour before you go out.

Note to this recipe: This tea has a very special magic quality. When a person drinks it, the scent of the blossoms is transferred into her sweat. The woman is perfumed from within, if you like, and the scent she gives off is irresistible to men. Naturally, it would be a shame to mask this intoxicating personal aroma with a synthetic fragrance. So for this one night you might consider doing without deodorants and perfumes.

Parisian Witch's Tea

This is a particularly effective recipe for bewitching men, and the effect is as hard to explain as it is spectacular. Any woman who has consumed this tea can twist any man around her little finger.

You will need a mysterious love herb with the Latin name *Circea lutetiana*, which means "Parisian witch." This plant of the nightshade family grows wild in many European mixed forests. You can recognize *Circea lutetiana* by its heart-shaped leaves and small white flowers, which later develop into little burrs. There are three varieties of the plant— small, medium and large—and all three are equally effective. You cannot buy the plant, however; a woman has to go and find it for herself. Of an evening when the moon is waxing or full, the woman must pick the flowers with her own hand, never taking the roots. She also has to leave some flowers, picking only from every second of third plant. She should hang the bunch of flowers to dry for ten days or two weeks.

Dried (or fresh) leaves of witch of Paris

Preparation and use: Whatever you can pinch between thumb, index finger and middle finger is the right amount for you. Brew this tea with 1 cup (250 ml) of boiling water and let it steep for 5 or 10 minutes. Strain and sweeten slightly. Before important events, drink a cup of this tea.

Notes to this recipe: Armed with this "attraction tea," a woman who is searching for a husband can conduct a focused campaign. You have to be careful, though: you will attract any

type of man, even guys who could turn out to be a nuisance. This witch's tea has proven most useful in situations where a female wanted to reach a specific goal with respect to a male, for example, a raise, a gift or the green light for her project. The herb is completely non-poisonous. In fact many women have been known to intensify its effect under certain circumstances by wearing it about their person, say, a few sprigs sewn into a jacket pocket or a flower spirited into a boot...

Because of the amazing results produced by this magic witch's herb, it is advisable to use some judgment in handling it. It is best to know, for example, that use of *Circea lutetiana* will evoke hostility from members of one's own sex. Thus it would be best to avoid its use at a conference where other women are also present. And do not try to use it to manipulate the boss's secretary: the attempt will end in abject failure.

Tea for Birth Magic

This recipe is "white magic" from the kitchens of good witches. In fact, since the Middle Ages, it has helped millions of women by easing their pain while birthing their babies. Today it is still regarded as a secret recipe by midwives with a herbalist orientation.

Vervain
Lady's mantle
Raspberry leaves

Preparation and use: Mix all 3 herbs in equal amounts. Per cup of boiling water, use 1 teaspoon of the blend. Steep for a few minutes before you strain it. Begin by drinking 1 cup of this tea per day 4 weeks before you are due. Increase the amount so that you are drinking close to a liter a day by the time of delivery.

Notes to this recipe: Midwives working in the context of naturopathy say that raspberry tea can prevent a breach during delivery. Lady's mantle has the virtue of regulating hormonal activity and purifying the blood. There are those who say that many a man would still have his wife and many a child would not be an orphan if women would drink more lady's mantle tea before and during childbirth. It is a good idea to continue to take the tea for a few days after the baby has been delivered, because it helps prevent infections. Moreover, it promotes the elasticity and rebuilding of the tissues.

Additional tip: When labor sets in, every woman should take a bath with either lavender or rosemary. If it is your first baby, reach for lavender; it will calm your system. For those who have given birth before, the energy-giving powers of rosemary will be more helpful; they will give you the strength to speed the work of birthing.

The way to put these herbs into a bath is to use aromatic oil. Mix about eight drops with a teaspoon of honey and add this to the bath as it is running. If you want to increase labor, add some tea of vervain to the bath as well.

ALCHEMY—THE MOTHER OF ALL SCIENCES

The only thing most people today know about the alchemists is that they tried to turn stone or metal into gold. This ignorance does not do justice to the craft of alchemy. Naturally, all the magicians and conjurors who used their art for this purpose failed miserably. The real alchemists, however, were highly aware human beings. They recognized that the physical and chemical processes of the laboratory were mere symbols for something of much greater significance. They were after the cosmic blueprint, the ultimate units of life. And they believed that the philosophers' stone could only be discovered by someone who had created it within himself.

Human Beings Must Walk the Path of "Elevation"

The goal of alchemy is indeed the transmutation or "the 'elevation' (*exaltatio*) and perfection of rock into gold," as the alchemist Marino Lazzeroni wrote shortly before his death. However, he made clear that in order for this to be achieved, mankind must also "walk the path of ennoblement." This implies "a change of such a high magnitude as to be scientifically and psychologically incomprehensible." The real alchemists were always great philosophers and scholars. "This science is open to very few people," says the modern-day physician Dagmar Lallinger-Bolling. "No one can comprehend it unless God or a master has opened his intellect." She adds that knowledge thus acquired may not be passed on to others, who may not be worthy of it. "Since all significant matters are expressed in terms of analogies, the message will only reach those who have the gift of understanding. The dense ones take things literally and are led astray by recipes."

These statements clarify what alchemy is about, namely, the expansion of "the far too narrow horizons of rational thinking" and entry into "the immense halls of analogous patterns of thought, which man can use to understand the wisdom of the cosmic order." To express it in much simpler terms, the alchemist must use both hemispheres of the brain to reach his elevated goals—the analytical left side and the intuitive right side, which opens up the way to the soul.

Paracelsus—A Great Alchemist

One of history's most important alchemists was the physician Paracelsus (1493–1541). He was born in Switzerland, the son of a doctor, and his real name was Theophrastus Bombastus von Hohenheim. He has been called a revolutionary intellectual pioneer in the field of natural science, to which he brought a holistic approach, and he is considered the founder of modern medicine. Paracelsus was the first to use the concept of "Spagyria." Today this is the part of alchemical teaching that deals with the art of healing. The word comes from the Greek and combines the roots *spaõ* (to separate) and *agairõ* (to bind). What is meant is the separation of matter into its basic elements and the creation of new connections according to the three basic principles of alchemy:

- separation (*separatio*)
- purification (*purificatio*)
- recombination (*cohobatio*)

Contemporary Revival

Two great alchemists of the twentieth century are responsible for the rebirth of interest in spagyrics: the mystical poet and thinker

Alexander von Bernus (1880–1965) and his spiritual heir, Marino Lazzeroni (1937–96). Baron Bernus became known as "the last of the mages." He was a philosophical and mystical poet, in constant correspondence with the great minds of his time. Among his close friends was Rudolf Steiner. Bernus was one of the first to recognize the limits of linear thought, which is adhered to by scientific medicine, a course that is coming under increasing criticism in our own day. Bernus made clear that scientific medicine has willfully chosen to focus exclusively on the lowest levels of reality and, as a consequence, has condemned itself to obtain only fragmented, unconnected facts. Only on the technical level—that is, in surgery—will medicine be able to achieve complete results. Comprehensive cures for major internal illnesses, by way of contrast, are possible only if medicine admits of a spiritual view of nature, which can grasp connections between the cosmic and physical levels of reality.

Bernus owned old alchemical recipe books written by Paracelsus, and he wanted to bring these up to date. In 1921 he founded a company he called Laboratorium Soluna in his own castle, Schloss Donaumünster near Donauwörth. His firm began making healing products, the spagyric tinctures. They were very successful. Bernus claimed that, "The healing effects of spagyrics approach the limits of credibility. They seem incredible only to people who approach them with the assumptions and prejudices of contemporary materialistic natural science."

In the early eighties the journalist Marino Lazzeroni arrived at Schloss Donaumünster and obtained the permission of Bernus's widow to browse among his recipes. Soon he recognized his calling. He explained it this way: "There is an urgent need today for what it took Bernus sixty-five years to achieve." Eighteen years after the death of the great master, Lazzeroni invested a great deal of money, and hired half a dozen people, in order to continue developing the spiritual heritage of Alexander von Bernus.

To this day, at the Laboratorium Soluna all the healing preparations are made strictly by the old recipes. The developing tinctures are agitated at sunrise in a direction and to a rhythm corresponding to the sun's energy; in the evening, at moonrise, they are stirred in the opposite direction and to a lunar rhythm. The rhythmical development of the spagyric healing products is slowly becoming known. From all over the continent of Europe, doctors come to visit the village.

The raw materials—the plants—used at the Saluna laboratories also meet the highest standards. They are collected in the wild or cultivated with great care, being sown, tended and harvested according to the biorhythms of the sun and moon. More and more alternative health practitioners and natural healers are making use of spagyric medications.

How Spagyrics Work

The procedures prescribed in the recipes for spagyrics, including the processes of separation, solution and purification, were created in faithful imitation of nature. The difference is that the transmutations of minerals, metals and plants that take place in nature follow great rhythms, while the procedures followed in the laboratory replicate these rhythms on a small scale, speeding them up by using various tools along with heat: distillation, sublimation and calcination.

The goal of this elaborate methodology is to enhance the effectiveness of the life force inherent in plants and minerals. This is achieved through repeated distillations. The distillate may be recombined with its own dregs and redistilled within the same closed system as many as thirty-three times. Through the constant changes in the state of the aggregate the substance itself is changed, in that its molecular energy is raised, its power heightened and a very high degree of purity attained. In the end, the active forces are actually separated from their material structures. They are beyond chemical analysis and can only be recognized by their actual healing effects. Healing is not achieved by the liquid but by the information it carries—the pure life force, separated from, and untouched by, matter.

In our day, with holistic medication—which treats body, soul and spirit—is once again coming into its own, spagyrics too is winning new adherents. The physician quoted earlier, Dagmar Lallinger-Bolling, says: "It is great that there is a medication that bears the secret of how to balance energies and the structures that form them."

The Spagyric Herbal Tinctures

To give a practical demonstration of the alchemical arts of healing, in this section we will introduce not plants but spagyric tinctures. You can order them from the suppliers listed at the back of this book. Nonetheless, it is a good idea to consult a practitioner who is familiar with these remedies because, as with so much else in medicine, "the secret is in [the size of] the dose."

Warning: The spagyric tinctures described here contain up to 65 percent alcohol. If you do not tolerate alcohol well, it is best to consult your physician before trying these tinctures.

Aquavit

Composition: A spagyric essence of angelica root, anise, cinchona bark, cola seeds, cubeb pepper, oregano, rootstock of galangal, ginger root, St. John's wort, coriander, caraway, lavender blossoms, marjoram, masterwort rootstock, melissa leaves, nutmeg "seeds," rosemary leaves, sage leaves, black pepper fruits, centaury, juniper berries, white pepper fruit, hyssop and cinnamon, in addition to gold salt (*aurum chloratum*) and an aqueous distillate of all the named drugs.

Aquavit is a classic elixir of life, said to vitalize mind and body and to reactivate the entire organism. According to spagyric experts, this life-enhancing effect of Aquavit is due to one special ingredient: the gold. Paracelsus wrote: "Gold is of the nature of fire. It carries the energy of the sun, ignites the love of life, strengthens the heart and quickens the blood, promotes growth, and grants greatness and power. Gold also carries the warmth that ripens all things." Aquavit combines the enlivening effect of gold salt with the spagyric essences of twenty-four healing plants, which also stimulate our metabolism. Yet the effect of Aquavit is by no means limited to the physical body; this strengthening tonic has a strong positive impact on the state of the soul. This spagyric tincture is able to dispel black moods and bring sunshine into our disposition. This is why it is an ingredient in the tea called Joy of Life, which you will find in the recipe section that follows. Aquavit as a tonic herbal tincture is recommended in all cases of weakness, whether after an illness or operation, in times of stress, or when we have lost courage and suffer from a general feeling of heaviness and lack of energy. Unless otherwise directed by a practitioner, take Aquavit 2 to 4 times daily by adding 5 to 10 drops and some sugar to a liqueur glass of wine or herbal tea.

Azinat

Composition: Liquid iron sugar, colloidal silicic acid, distillate of *Stibium sulfuratum nigrum* in ethanol, *Stibium sulfuratum nigrum* and sodium nitrate in purified water, *Tartarus stibiatus D3 aquos*, purified water.

Azinat is a fundamental spagyric remedy that mobilizes the immune system. Medical research into its application has been going on now for sixty years, and the most impressive successes achieved with Azinat seem to occur with acute inflammatory processes. Azinat helps the body to react to external attacks in an efficient manner. Illnesses of the respiratory system, with or without fever, are where this particular herbal tincture is most commonly applied. Other diseases involving inflammation are relieved by it too, for example arthritis of the joints and disturbances of the glandular system and of the skin.

At the first sign of a cold or flu take 30 drops of Azinat as soon as possible. You can add it to a cup of yarrow or horsetail tea. After that alternate every 2 hours between 10 drops of Azinat and 10 drops of Epidemic. Continue for 18 to 24 hours. During the following 3 to 6 days, depending on the progress of your condition, increase the interval between treatments. Do continue taking the tincture for several days after all your symptoms have disappeared.

Dyscrasin N

Composition: Spagyric essence from a distillate of *Stibium sulfuratum nigrum* with ethanol, antimony iodide D4 in ethanol, essential oils of cajeput, cedar wood and turpentine, *Terebinthinae sulf. eath.*

The name of this tincture derives from a medical concept developed by Hippocrates, *dyskrasie*, which refers to a faulty constitution of the bodily humors. The term indicates a complex of symptoms that contemporary medicine would describe as "allergic, exudative-lymphatic diathesis"—in plain English, a hereditary or acquired tendency to pathological reaction by certain organs or organ systems. Dyscratic symptoms include neuro-dermatitic eczema, psoriasis or acne. All of these diseases are symptoms of deeper metabolic dysfunction. Dyscrasin N aims at the direct detoxification of the affected organs or organ systems, the impurities of which are given off through the skin.

To treat acne, eczema or scrofula, 5 to 8 drops of the tincture are usually taken 2 or 3 times a day. However, because individuals differ in their needs and because the dose is often increased during the course of the treatment, it is best to consult a health practitioner.

Epidemic

Composition: Colloidal silicic acid, *Stibium sulfuratum nigrum* in ethanol, *Stibium sulfuratum nigrum* and sodium nitrate in purified water, *Tartarus stibiatus D3 aquos*, purified water.

Adherents of spagyrics claim that in this remedy physicians are offered a very effective "probiotic" against diseases that are normally treated with antibiotics. This applies to all acute and subacute infectious diseases, with or without fever. With acute infections such as influenza, Epidemic acts as a powerful febrifuge. The tincture achieves this by strengthening humorous and cellular factors, thus enabling the body to

counteract the infection. In other words, unlike allopathic medicine, which would suppress the fever, the principle at work here supports the body in resisting it and overcoming it more efficiently. The efficacy of Epidemic has also been proven with diseases of a subacute or chronic nature, where an infection seems to smolder on and on. Children seem particularly susceptible to getting stuck for years with such subacute infectious conditions; think of the constantly running nose or the chronic little cough. Such low-level infections are always a sign of incipient immune system weakness.

Epidemic, the immune system booster, complements the effects of Azinat, and the two remedies should really be taken in tandem, alternating one with the other. Dosage is best determined by an expert in this area.

Hepatic

Composition: Spagyric essence of scarlet pimpernel, kapaloe, quasia bark (*Simarouba excelsa*), noble agrimony (*Anemone hepatica*), dandelion (whole plant), milk thistle fruit, common agrimony (*Agrimonia eupatoria*), root of greater celandine, wild chicory leaves, wild chicory root and zinc acetate, plus an aqueous distillate of all the drugs listed.

As the name indicates, this is a remedy for our most important organ of detoxification, the liver. Hepatic has three great healing properties, which make it effective for the entire range of liver–gallbladder problems: it decongests, reduces inflammation and supports the liver's ability to regenerate itself. Evidently, Hepatic can be used in many different situations, ranging from incipient disorders of the organs of digestion to fully manifested damage to the organs,

including gallstones, inflammations of the gallbladder and all forms of liver dysfunction. Furthermore, this spagyric remedy is so complex that it can also be employed with equal success in preventative therapy for the protection of the liver.

All nine of the healing herbs contained in this tincture have been used since time immemorial for the treatment of liver disease. They are known to free up the flow of fluids through the liver and to carry off the toxins that collect there as a result of congestion. A very important component of this tincture is the spagyrically treated zinc. The close connection of this trace element to the health and functioning of the liver has been documented by modern scientific research. We know that the detoxifying and immunological tasks of the liver are catalyzed by zinc.

In his own time Paracelsus, the creator of spagyrics, recognized this connection, though by non-scientific means. Taoist and anthroposophical medicine have also come to the same awareness. When taking Hepatic, it is particularly important to consult an expert, since the dose is adjusted to the reaction of each patient. The amount prescribed is usually increased over a longer treatment period. The tincture is most effective if added to a tea of wild chicory.

Lymphatic N

Composition: Spagyric essence of lignum vitae (*Guaiacum officinale*), red sandalwood, sarsaparilla root, absinthium (*Artemisia absinthium*), walnut leaves, and an aqueous distillate of these plants and plant parts.

Lymphatic N is usually employed against disorders of the lymph glands, skin diseases and metabolic disturbances. The remedy has a normalizing effect on the entire lymph system. The tincture is prescribed together with Dyscrasin N in cases of so-called "lymphatic diathesis," which is frequently found in people who suffer from skin diseases. The plants listed above further the excretion of lymphatic fluids from the connective tissues and all the lymphatic organs they contain, as well as from the adjacent mucous membranes. Lymphatic N can improve the overall maintenance of the body's tissues. Through the general purification and renewal of the skin that this process involves, we often find cosmetic improvements following healing.

Four to eight drops, twice daily, is the usual recommended dose. To support its work it is a good idea to take the prescribed number of drops of Lymphatic N in a blood-purifying tea. Where the skin condition is a hereditary disease, Lymphatic N should be combined with Dyscrasin N. An expert in spagyric medicine should prescribe the doses.

Stomachic

Composition: Spagyric essence of angelica root, mugwort, gentian root, rootstock of sweet galingale, calamus rootstock, masterwort rootstock, melissa leaves, peppermint leaves, orange peel, rosemary leaves, centaury, juniper berries, wormwood herb, and an aqueous distillate of all of these plants and plant parts.

This stomach remedy relieves all non-inflammatory digestive problems, such as pressure on the stomach, burping, nausea, bloating, and all problems associated with nervous stomach and intestines. The thirteen plants, many of them classic stomach herbs, act in a cumulative manner; that is to say, the spagyric distillation causes their various effects to build on one another. The range of healing powers offered by the many plants in this tincture allows the most appropriate plant to deliver its healing action, with the other plants adding their own special slant to increase the main medication's effectiveness. All in all, Stomachic relaxes the entire digestive system, right down to the gallbladder, stimulates stomach juices and relieves the symptoms of a sour stomach. It is best to take the tincture after meals; the dose is 5 to 10 drops in a teaspoon of tea, wine or sugar.

ALCHEMICAL HEALING POTIONS FOR EVERYDAY COMPLAINTS

The recipes in this section were developed by Anna-Elisabeth Röcker, a healing practitioner in Munich, who has been working successfully with spagyrics for many years.

Joy of Life Tea

When our lives are not joyful and we are lacking any élan, according to the theories of spagyrics we are suffering from a disturbance of the sun principle. Depression causes all the problems of life to appear more serious than they actually are. People who are in this state worry day and night. The best therapy is these cases is light—in all its forms, on all levels.

The plants that heal dark moods do so by contributing the light that is stored in them. Astrologically, they are all subordinate to the sun. The best example is St. John's wort (*Hypericum perforatum*). It is in full bloom at the summer solstice and is harvested only during the light-filled days of that time of year. St. John's wort is one of the best-known and most extensively researched herbal remedies for depression. The drops of Aquavit tincture that are part of the tea recipe below act as a general revitalizer for the entire system. Aquavit's most important active ingredient is gold, that is, a spagyric preparation of real gold, which is able to return the sun's light to our psyche. This life elixir can be used by itself any time you feel low in spirits or experience general physical weakness, as after an operation or giving birth.

> 0.7 oz. (20 g) elder blossoms
> 1 oz. (50 g) St. John's wort
> 1 oz. (30 g) mullein (Verbascum thrapsus)
> 1 oz. (30 g) cornflower (Centaurea cyanus)
> 0.7 oz. (20 g) genuine bedstraw (Galium)

> 2 oz. (50 g) honigklee
> c. 1 cup (200 ml) water
> 1 bottle Aquavit

Preparation and Use: Mix all the tea herbs very well. To prepare the tea, pour the boiling water over 2 teaspoons of the blend and cover immediately. Let stand 5 minutes, then strain. Drink 2 large cups of this tea per day, sweetened with some honey if you like. Just before drinking it, add 10 drops of Aquavit to the tea, so that you are taking a total of 20 drops a day. Keep up this Joy of Life therapy for about 6 weeks. You have to make fresh tea each time.

Note to this recipe: If you happen to suffer from low blood pressure, it is good to substitute the spagyric tincture Sanguisol, which contains—in addition to gold—substances that will stimulate your circulation and your heart.

Warning: Joy of Life Tea alone is not sufficient therapy for true, clinical depression. It can be used, however, to support medical treatment. Other useful remedies for depression include physical exercise in general and the hatha yoga sequence called Salute to the Sun.

Digestive Tea

Most people's digestive system is overstressed because we all tend to eat and drink too often, too much and too many different foods, some of them not particularly good for us. Conversely, since human beings are complete entities consisting of mind, soul and body, extreme pressures of a nervous or psychological nature will affect the digestion in a negative way. Classic symptoms are heartburn, burping, a feeling of pressure or bloating after eating, and tendencies to diarrhea or constipation.

0.7 oz. (20 g) angelica root
0.7 oz. (20 g) calamus
0.4 oz. (10 g) melissa leaves
0.4 oz. (10 g) strawberry leaves
1 cup (250 ml) water
a bottle of Stomachic 1 tincture
or *a bottle of Hepatic tincture*

Preparation and use: Add a heaping teaspoon of this mixture to the boiling water, cover the pot and allow the tea to steep for 15 minutes. Drink a cup of this tea after lunch and another after dinner. As for the spagyrics, use them as follow:

- If nervousness affects your stomach and you tend to experience the typical symptoms of tension, such as burping, nausea or a disagreeable pressure on the stomach, add to your tea 7 to 10 drops of Stomachic, and drink each cup after meals.
- If your problem is bloating and constipation, it is better to take Hepatic, which will address the symptoms through the liver and gallbladder.

If you wish, you can start with 10 drops per cup twice a day and increase it to 15 drops over

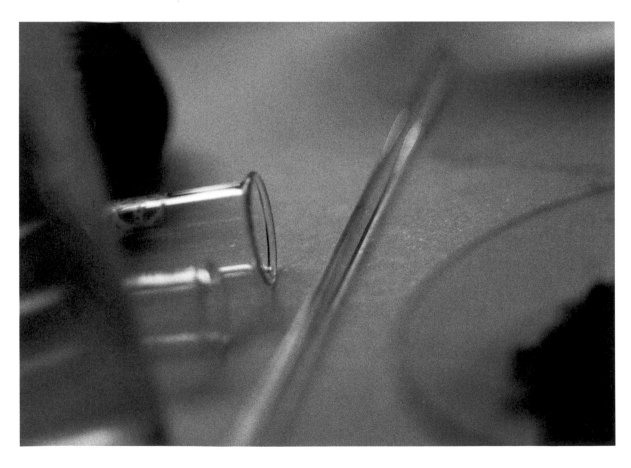

time. If you take a lot of laxatives, your dosage will have to be a bit higher. You can remain on this digestive therapy for a maximum of 6 weeks. Make your tea fresh each day.

Spagyric Purification Therapy for Body and Soul

Do you often feel tired and dragged out? Do you suffer from joint diseases, allergies or skin problems? Do you carry too much body weight? Are you often in a bad mood? Do you tend to see the dark side of things? Any of these symptoms indicates that your body retains waste materials. Through daily doses of pesticides, fertilizers and additives, our environment delivers into our system a range of toxins, which we duly store in various locations. In order not to perish from these poisons, every adult should undertake a cleansing therapy once or twice a year, say, in the spring and the fall. The recipe here given helps the body to dispose of harmful metabolic by-products. If you stay with it for 6 weeks, you will feel newly born: vital, lighthearted, free of physical and mental heaviness. Even dark moods and black thoughts will vanish, as if blown away. This spagyric tea detoxification is particularly effective if combined with a fast (tea or juice fast) or therapeutic diet, for example the F. X. Mays diet. Naturally, the spagyric therapy works without this extra step. It is best, however, to make sure that you eat a healthy, light diet and avoid coffee and alcohol while you are taking this tea.

0.7 oz. (20 g) stinging nettle
0.7 oz. (20 g) dandelion root and herb
0.4 oz. (10 g) horsetail
0.2 oz. (5 g) birch leaves
0.2 oz. (5 g) rosehips, including the seeds
2 cups (500 ml) water
1 bottle Hepatic (to relieve the liver)
1 bottle Lymphatic N (for inner lymph drainage)
1 bottle Renalin (to detoxify the kidneys)

Preparation and use: Add 4 heaping table-spoons of the tea mixture to 2 cups (500 ml) boiling water, cover and let steep for 15 minutes. Strain and store in a Thermos bottle. This is your daily dose of tea and the basis for the three spagyric purification tinctures. The amount of the tinctures you take depends on whether or not you are also fasting during this therapeutic period.

- If you are not fasting, drink a cup on an empty stomach in the morning, another at noon and another in the evening, before dinner. To your morning cup of tea add 15 drops of Lymphatic, to your pre-lunch cup add 15 drops of Renalin and to your evening cup add 15 drops of Hepatic.
- If you are fasting, you will have to dilute the tinctures quite a lot, since they contain alcohol. Add the following daily dose to your Thermos bottle and drink the tea over the course of the day:
  The first day's dose: 20 drops Lymphatic
  The second day's dose: 20 drops Renalin
  The third day's dose: 20 drops Hepatic.
  On the fourth day proceed as on the first, on the fifth, as on the second, and so on, rotating through the three tinctures.

Note to this recipe: If you prefer a finished tea to making your own blend, Salus sells a very good substitute called Blood Purification Tea, Herbal Tea #7. It comes as loose tea or in bags.

Prescription for a Cold

A frequently recurring cold is always an indication of a weakened immune system; a healthy body has no problem dealing with the ever-present germs in its normal environment. It is true, however, that the transitional seasons—spring and fall—always put special stress on the body, rendering it more vulnerable. The prescription that follows is designed to serve you either when you feel a cold coming on or when the cold is already fully developed.

The tea blend is made of equal parts of the following:

Lungwort (Sticta pulmonaria)
Coltsfoot
Sage
¾ cup (200 ml) water
1 Bottle Azinat (for an incipient cold)
or *1 bottle Pulmonic and*
1 bottle Epidemic (for a cold in progress)

Preparation and use: Pour the boiling water over 3 teaspoons of the tea blend and let the tea steep for 10 minutes. Drink 3 cups of it over the course of the day. For the prevention or elimination of a slight cold, place about 5 drops of Azinat into each cup you drink. This tincture strengthens the body's defenses and helps your system fight the invaders.

When the symptoms of flu are present, and you have a fever, runny nose, cough or bronchial irritation, then 5 to 10 drops each of Pulmonic and Epidemic should be put into each cup of tea. This tea therapy can be supplemented with other appropriate measures, such as a cottage cheese poultice: Place a thick layer of cold, well-drained cottage cheese on a thin cloth and lay it over your chest. Remove the poultice when the cottage cheese is quite warm. You can repeat this as needed.

Note to this recipe: The tea mixture above can be replaced successfully by the ready-to-buy tea from Salus called Chest Cough Tea, Herbal Tea No. 9.

Skin Elixir with Pansies

This adjustable recipe helps all those with skin problems, but especially people who have to cope with acne, pimples and oily skin. The elixir is also recommended for other skin diseases, like psoriasis, eczema, and fungal infections of the skin or feet. A footbath of the tea is recommended against foot infections. Affected areas can be treated with grapefruit seed extract and tea tree oil to relieve symptoms.

3 tbsp. dried herb of pansy
2 cups (500 ml) water
1 bottle Lymphatic
1 bottle Dyscrasin

Preparation and use: Cover the herb with hot but not boiling water and let it sit for 10 minutes before you strain it. This makes enough for 3 cups, which is the daily dose. Place in each cup of tea 5 drops of Lymphatic and 3 drops of Dyscrasin. If you are able to stick to this tea regime for 8 full weeks, you should be able to rejoice at your new complexion.

Note to this recipe: To support the effect of this tea therapy you can do compresses or facial masks with the pansy tea. Before applying the compress, you might wish to rub your skin lightly with a cut lemon. Soak a cloth in the lukewarm tea and place it on your skin.

To make a facial mask blend cottage cheese, lemon juice and the tea, and place the mixture on your face.

Spagyric Hot Flash Tea

Even though the majority of women between forty-five and fifty-five have no serious problems with menopause, their well-being might still be affected by hot flashes or mood swings. A mild corrective for such cases is supplied by this spagyric tea for hot flashes; the active ingredient is supplied by the phytoestrogen in the sage.

0.7 oz. (20 g) sage leaves
2 oz. (50 ml) water
1 bottle Matrigen II
1 bottle Aquavit
1 bottle Cerebretik

Preparation and use: The amounts given for water and sage suffice for a single cup of tea; you will have to make the tea fresh every morning and evening. Enrich your morning cup with 10 drops of Matrigen II and 15 drops of Aquavit. To the cup you drink in the evening add 10 drops of Matrigen II as before, but also add 10 to 15 drops of Cerebretik.

Note to this recipe: You can substitute other, ready-made menopause teas for the tea of sage. Be careful, however, to choose teas that contain plants with a mild, gentle phytohormonal action. Among these are, in addition to sage, chaste tree or monk's pepper (*Vitex*), false unicorn root (*Chamaelirium luteum*), wild yam root, hops and licorice. You can support the work of the herbs by avoiding coffee and alcohol. What also helps are a base (i.e., alkaline) powder mixture and a low-salt diet.

INDEX